DIPTYCH

DIPTYCH

CERDDI · POEMS

R. GERALLT JONES

CYHOEDDIADAU MODERN CYMREIG/
MODERN WELSH PUBLICATIONS

I wlad Llŷn:
yno y gorwedd gwreiddiau'r cyfan

Published in 2012 by
Modern Welsh Publications
of Allerton, Liverpool

Cyhoeddwyd yn 2012 gan
Cyhoeddiadau Modern Cymreig
32 Garth Drive, Lerpwl L18 6HW

ISBN 978 1 84323 710 5

Argraffwyd a rhwymwyd yng Nghymru gan
Wasg Gomer, Llandysul, Ceredigion.

Diolchiadau

Mae fy nyled yn fawr iawn i Dr D. Ben Rees am ymgymryd â'r gwaith o gyhoeddi'r llyfr dwy-ieithog hwn. Carwn ddiolch hefyd i'r Athro Walford Davies a'r Athro Bobi Jones am eu cyfraniadau grymus. Rwyf yn ddiolchgar i bawb, enwedig i Dafydd, a fu o gymorth i mi wrth ddod a'r gwaith i fwcwl.

Acknowledgements

I wish to express my deep gratitude to Dr D. Ben Rees for undertaking this bilingual publication. My thanks go to Professor Walford Davies and Professor Bobi Jones for their considerable contributions. I am grateful to all, especially Dafydd, who helped and encouraged me in this work.

SŴ GERALLT JONES

Cynnwys / Contents

Preface

This is a selection of translations of his own poems by R. Gerallt Jones, face-to-face with the original Welsh. In theme and form poems, in both languages, will speak for themselves. If any wider introduction were needed, its most appropriate form would be the poet's own acute statement, 'The Problems of Translation', which is also included here. Honoured by the invitation to write a Preface to a volume by so fine a writer, I know it can be only a small part of the full context. Gerallt himself, whom I was privileged to know over many years as a friend and colleague, I shall return to.

Terms of translation of poetry vary. One attempt may be called a 'version', another an 'imitation', while another might be described as 'after' or 'from' such-and-such by so-and-so. The only thing a poem cannot be is simply 'transferred' – the Latin root of the word 'translated'. And with all types of rendering the very act of translating is further controlled and edited at both ends by the two languages involved. An honourable and useful tradition exists of aiming at something as nose-to-nose as possible, short-sightedly as at a mirror, though that is to be optimistic about even what we see in mirrors, and is only really justifiable when we're translating prose, *into* prose, for its discursive sense alone. Robert Frost's claim that 'poetry is what is lost in translation' has become a bit of a cliché, but it remains a challenge, not a jibe. Frost wasn't denying the possibility of an *equivalent* poetry being stimulated in the new language. Anyway, Frost's view of the matter is mild compared to some others. Asked whether he read foreign poetry, Philip Larkin's reply was 'Foreign *poetry*? No!', and again dismissively, 'If that glass thing over there is a window, then it isn't a Fenester or a fenêtre or whatever. Hautes Fenêtres, my God!' Larkin's prejudiced splutterings and what he called his 'hatred of abroad' are odd for such an intelligent man and fine poet. Did he actually think it a good thing to go through life with absolutely no knowledge of Vergil or Dante or Rilke? Or of Dafydd ap

Gwilym or T. H. Parry Williams or Waldo Williams or R. Gerallt Jones? – for sadly, Welsh-language poetry too is *terra incognita* to the vast majority of Britishers. Larkin's 'fenester' wasn't even a stab at Welsh *ffenestr*.

'Hautes Fenêtres' – Larkin was of course cynically translating the title of his last volume, High Windows. The phrase is, accidentally, a good image for the isolationism that refuses to read 'foreign' poetry even in translation. It is the result of a needlessly super-charged, unnegotiable nationalism. In another Larkin poem, 'The Importance of Elsewhere', the 'elsewhere' is in fact England, described as the 'elsewhere' that he carries with him and which 'underwrites' his existence whenever he has to be somewhere outside England. On the importance of having one's own cultural rootedness Larkin is of course right: we have to have a native 'somewhere' in our writing and our reading, just as in our general lives, even if 'being native' is itself not without its complications and divisions. But we should not forget that the world's other countries – what we *normally* call 'elsewhere' – have their own excellent literatures. For too many of us those literatures are as good as non-existent without translation. It is worth adding that Larkin himself, of course, is a copiously-translated poet.

The conviction that poetry translation enriches us world-wide has had new impetus and manifestation in the last half century. The act of translation – that special crossing of borders – was always a deeply radical act, and in our own time it continues to promote literally inter-national understanding through a democracy of the imagination. Its quiet lines of communication were amongst the peaceful forces that helped bring down the Berlin Wall, and the delight of translation as an art in itself has had enthusiastic championing in practice as well as theory from such major, highly individualistic poets of our time as Ted Hughes, Geoffrey Hill and Seamus Heaney. From the increased welcome given to translated poems in our periodicals – whether 'version', 'imitation', 'after' or 'from' – we have benefited in learning about the 'elsewheres' where others live. We also have the increasing influence of that excellent publication *Modern Poetry in Translation* and of the dedication of the 'Stephen Spender Prize' specifically to Poetry

Translation. Newly established in Wales we have the annual Translation Prize of Translators' House Wales (Tŷ Cyfieithu Cymru).

With his capacious volume of translations, *Poetry of Wales 1930–70* (1974), Gerallt was an early partner and shaping spirit in this development in Wales. But in the present volume what we have is the Welshman exclusively translating his own poems. He did so into an English he was equally at home in (the version and the original are comfortably face-to-face, not nose-to-nose), in a nation that ideally should be at home in Welsh as well as in English, but unhappily isn't. Yet translating his poems for non-Welsh-speaking readers inside Wales has no different aims from doing so outside Wales, and beyond. Naturally, for Welsh-language readers anywhere, experiencing the poems in Welsh will probably remain the starting point for the enjoyment of this volume as a whole. But even for Welsh-language readers, the translations will open up a door on the imagination that made the original poems possible. To 'open up' a door is a more radical act than opening a door; it is to create a new doorway. As such it is a better image for the act of translation than the idea of a window. A poem, whether original or translated, is something one in a sense 'enters'. A sensitive translation makes perceptible the shape, proportions, furniture and atmosphere of the original. It is not just a glimpse through glass.

Gerallt's background and career were varied. They were also faceted in unexpected ways. One of the outstanding Welsh-language writers of his generation, he was the son of the vicarage, not of the manse, the product of private schools in England, not of the local schools of his native Llŷn, a graduate (at Bangor University) in English, not Welsh, and the author there of a research thesis on Robert Graves. After a period as a school-teacher, he became a university lecturer in Education at Aberystwyth University, then founding Principal of a College of Education in Jamaica (the start of a personal outreach that was to encompass many continents, notably India and the former Soviet world). Back in Wales, after a period as the headmaster (Warden) of Llandovery College, he became Senior Lecturer in Aberystwyth University's Department of Extra-Mural Studies, and then the enlightened administrator as Warden of the University of Wales's Gregynog Hall. All along, his inestimable contribution as member of institutions such as the Arts Council of Wales and the Welsh Academy drew on his commitment to wider fields in the arts beyond literature, notably film, drama and television. Further, the Welsh poet, who was at the same time a published poet in English, was also an acclaimed novelist and scriptwriter. Manifestly, his urbane and perceptive publications as a literary critic were, to use T. S. Eliot's words, the 'product' of the 'workshop' of his own creative writing.

Gerallt's involvement in so many aspects of imaginative life always seemed to me the practice of a joyous morality. He seemed to embody in his very person what it is like to live a complete life of tireless creativity. I know he would have agreed with the words of that most private of poets, Gerard Manley Hopkins. They are somewhat unexpected in coming from a poet who settled for leaving his own work unpublished in his lifetime. That makes it all the more selfless and honourable that he should commend to others the pleasant duty of making all creative work widely known. As such, Hopkins's words are also relevant to the whole purpose of translation:

> What are works of art for? To educate, to be standards. Education is meant for the many, standards are for public use. To produce then is of little use unless what we produce is known, if known widely known, the wider known the better, for it is by being known it works, it influences, it does its duty, it does good. We must then try to be known, aim at it, take means to it.

WALFORD DAVIES

Introduction

Inevitably, in taking up a book of translations, particularly when it includes a parallel copy in the original Welsh, the reader will anticipate a duality of some sort. One language will confront the other in tension yet with some sort of agreement.

The particular path followed in translating these poems, however, is rather exceptional and perhaps more interesting than usual. It involves a process that I have called 'Source Translation', and is quite different from the more conventional method adopted by the same translator himself when dealing with other people's work in his anthology *Poetry of Wales 1930–1970*. It may even remind us of Gerallt's own rather unique background.

Even before he began to put this present collection of translations together, he had himself already been obliged to face up to another, quite different, altogether more disturbing, duality in his own life. The practice of writing in two languages, something done by an occasional foreign writer such as Beckett, is not unknown in Wales. But in Gerallt's case, it involved a parallel crisis in the life of some of the nation besides himself. There was some sort of conversion, a reclamation, or even a complexity in some quarters on a communal level. And Gerallt's life itself, in a certain sense, had been likewise translated and reflected this.

In his case, as readers will suspect when they become acquainted with Gerallt's character in this volume, such duality was rather a gentle and civilised relationship not easily identifiable, but it was certainly some sort of rebirth.

I can imagine a newcomer to Welsh literature supposing that R. Gerallt Jones's Welsh credentials were somewhat tenuous. Baptised 'Gerald', the son of an Anglican priest, he was educated in a Public School in England. At University he studied English, and did his postgraduate treatise on the work of the early twentieth century English poet and novelist Robert Graves. He then became an English master at the beginning of his career at Amlwch, Principal of a teacher's training college in Jamaica and appointed Head of an English-medium public school – Llandovery College. Amongst his literary works was – albeit in Welsh – a very fine study of the work of T. S. Eliot. But he published a number of other books in the English language including *Jamaican Landscape* (poems) 1969 and *Jamaica Interlude*, 1977, besides (ed.) *Poetry of Wales* 1930–1970 and *The Welsh Literary Revival*, 1966, *A Study of the work of T. H. Parry-Williams*, followed by *A Place in the mind* 2004.

Altogether, he was well set to be a true blue English writer; which he was . . . and was obviously not. But even subsequently as one of the most prominent of our Welsh-language poets between the late sixties and the end of the last century, his style and presence were certainly not 'typically' Welsh. He belonged to a group of poets, including Professors Alun Llywelyn-Williams and Gareth Alban Davies whose verse was urbane and sophisticated, seemingly untraditional and modernist, not too far removed in atmosphere, it would seem, from the English and wider European trends upheld by their contemporaries. It was hardly a reflection of rural and pastoral, late romantic work still being trundled out by the conservatives in Welsh eisteddfodau. As a public figure, highly respected in the Media, Educational, Ecclesiastical and Arts spheres, Gerallt was finally awarded an OBE as if he were an ordinary member of the Establishment, although I suspect that he and others understood such an 'imperialist gesture' as paradoxical because of his non-imperialist poetry.

Such an institutional impression would be utterly incongruous.

Indeed his work in and on Welsh literature itself has been most substantial. True: he came as an 'outsider'. Fortunately for those of us who have come more directly to this field, it has been a great acquisition that he shared this duality with formidable scholars in other humanities, such as Dewi Z. Phillips, M. Wynn Thomas and Glyn Tegai Hughes. Having studied in other fields, their fresh vision and influential contributions have vitalised both Welsh creative and scholarly work. And Gerallt belonged to that noble company.

In many ways, translations from his work particularly in the eyes of the average non-Welsh reader could seem quite unexpected and extraordinary. His consciousness of identity, roots, and tradition, the perils of existence, the necessity of praise in a sceptic and jaded environment, all mark his verse out as belonging to an altogether different milieu from the run-of-the-mill modernist pattern. And I must try to explain this Welsh individualism. Gerallt was brought up in a Welsh-speaking and a Welsh-literate household in the strongest Welsh area in Wales. From 1959 till his death in 1999 he published in Welsh five volumes of poetry, five novels, one collection of short stories, six books of literary criticism, including a biography of Parry-Williams (published posthumously, but his best work of criticism), apart from one of the finest drama series seen on Welsh television, as well as numerous essays on places. He co-edited in turn two literary journals – *Yr Arloeswr* and *Taliesin*. He was appointed a University lecturer through the medium of Welsh several times in two separate departments, and eventually became Warden of the well-known cultural and conference-orientated University centre of Gregynog.

His poetic work, as so often happens with poets, can be viewed as a development over two specific periods. In the first two volumes *Ymysg y Drain* (1959) and *Cwlwm* (1962) he examined his own lyrical identity. The following *Cysgodion* (1972) and *Dyfal Gerddwyr y Maes* (1981) as well as additional verse in his *Welsh Collected Poems Cerddi 1955–1989* reflect his consciousness of a very self-critical social self, meditative and challenging. This, perhaps, is not unusual. But it seems to me what is fairly unusual from a non-Welsh perspective would be the presence and multiplicity of 'straight praise-poems' of people. The Welsh praise tradition of men and women since the sixth century should by our time have become more ironic, sceptical, dry in the industrial twentieth century environment as it did with R. S. Thomas for instance. Generally, Modernism and particularly Post-modernism had some difficulty in confronting genuinely sincere praise poems dedicated to human beings. Somehow, critical satire might be in order, even compulsory. And of course, in this Welsh tradition, there's a great deal of satire, and biting sarcasm. But in the twentieth century, that – together with portraits of wretched or lunatic specimens of humanity – almost became the stereotype art order of the day. But Gerallt really belonged to the central and defining tradition of direct praise. The stream of personal praise-poems began for him with 'I Hen Wraig' (For an Old Lady), 1956, and henceforth there never was a real let-up. There's a bunch of splendid praise-poems each to fellow patients in *Cwlwm*, then a number dedicated to fellow poets such as Alun Llywelyn-Williams, Derek Walcott, Goronwy Owen, two to Waldo, another to Ewan Mclachlan and quite a few to what we may count as craftsmen and ordinary folk. All an unusually positive celebration.

Just as significant are the place-poems, not just Aber-ffraw, Porth Dinllaen, Rhos-y-bol, Enlli, Porth Ceiriad, Llanbedrog, Ynys-Las, Mynydd Rhiw, Dô1-y-bont, Llanymddyfri, Hereford-shire, but Ennismore, Connemara, Paris, Galway, Santa Cruz, Rio Bueno, Arles, Menez Hom, Shetland, and Georgia. Their significance lies in the fact that most of these are related to people and to a past that is still experienced as a present, to a thrusting tradition even. In what I consider the best study of Gerallt Jones's work (in *Patrwm Amryliw* 2006), Alan Llwyd of Cyhoeddiadau Barddas discusses the poem 'Cytiau'r Gwyddelod', a hill fort on Garn Fadrun in Llŷn, which the poet relates to the worshipping carried on in tiny churches scattered here and there around the hill. The poet finds himself very much alive to the grip of a membrance of his ancestors, soldiers maybe, workers certainly who had created a civilisation here, a pattern of hedges, a community, with death wandering in and out of the generations, all knowing when to close the gate, how to build up gaps in the hedges, and the presence of cemeteries, all linked to 'Belief' during an age of Barbarism. One thing that drew Alan Llwyd's penetrative attention was the direct references to lines of verse by former poets related to this place – Rhys Cain (d.1641) and Siôn Phylip (c.1543-1620). This, I think, is a pretty general characteristic of other Welsh poetry. It is a poetry steeped in roots. I remember once driving through Ceredigion and just nodding in the direction of this and that place, hardly thinking about them. My companion, an Anglo-Welsh poet, mentioned as we got towards the end, how amazed he had been at the scores of important cultural points in our rich history that we had passed. Some of them literary, others military, others of religious significance, so much that he had known little about, and had certainly not learnt about at school or University, a complete rich tradition of which he had been bereft, having previously a consciousness of a Wales that was completely dead to him except for the twentieth century. Just in this county, we would pass the birthplace of our national Saint Dewi, (who had been the crux of the religious revival in the teeth of Pelagianism, a movement that had a strong influence on Ireland, Scotland, Cornwall and Brittany between the fifth and twelfth centuries); the birthplace of one of the foremost European poets of the fourteenth century, Dafydd ap Gwilym; the most solid scholar of Welsh literature during the Enlightenment, namely Ieuan Fardd; and one of the most intellectually gifted preachers in the experiential reformation of Christianity in the eighteenth century, Daniel Rowland; besides the base for an important military attack and possession of Aberystwyth castle by Glyndwr's army. All this, apart from the part played by half a dozen major scholars in the advance of Welsh literature during the first half of the twentieth century. This for him had been deafeningly mute. He knew nothing of their significance, just an oversimplified psychological awareness of nothing, an experience that had been, for too many monoglot Welsh people, the norm. For Gerallt, on the other hand, Welsh places were vibrant and vital everywhere in his work. He even wrote a biography of one of the characters I have just mentioned.

True: both Rhys Cain and Siôn Phylip wrote work in the cynghanedd form of verse, a very intricate patterning, sometimes known as the 'strict metres' (to be contrasted with so-called 'free-verse' of most European poetry). Actually, the metres are no more strict than the rest. The salient difference is not the strictness required in metrics. Strictness lay more specifically in the quality of the relationship between syllabic characteristics (vowels and consonants), rather than in easy accent-relationships. Gerallt was never a writer of cynghanedd, although there are touches of its influence here and there in his work: such as

(Tom)
Hiraethus, clwyfus ei liw . . .
Heddiw'n garedig i'r ydau

(Alcemi'r Gerdd)
Pwyawdr a chymrwd yn dylino powdrau
iaith, o gilfachau llwch ei silffoedd . . .

o'r frwynen y fronfraith, o'r waun y wennol,
a lliwiau cerdd yn lliniaru'r glew. Ar fore glân . . .

and much else.

Gerallt found himself using suggestions of Cynghanedd, and
gradually celebrating its force as a way of thinking. And Alan
Llwyd, the star poet of the 70s Cynghanedd revival and a brilliant
critic himself, warmed to Gerallt's work and published the best
essay on Gerallt's poems that we have up to now, changing his
response somewhat between 1986 and 1989/2006 with his usual
generous catholicity. Both sides were more complex and nuanced
than many had supposed. And perhaps the serene and slackly
leisurely pace of some of Gerallt's vers libre gradually appeared
more attractive to those favouring rather tight and dense word-
combinations of Cynghanedd. In other words, there was a sort of
reciprocal maturation. And eventually, Gerallt's *Collected Poems*
and other work were published by Barddas itself.

One little known item in Gerallt's bibliography, the collector's
item, Guto'r Glyn, Tern Press, 1976 (an edition of 100) is
testimony to his knowledge and real interest in the 'Great
Century' of Welsh poetry – namely the fifteenth.

In his poem 'Tai Duon' he loves simply to name and roll the
sound of places about his tongue with their recollections of
battles and prayers, finding himself at night tied up in his own
roots. And habitual Welsh echoes accompany his mind as he
journeyed through Wales in his appreciation of other resurgent
nations, particularly Ireland.

Thus, although Gerallt was not a controversial figure in Welsh
Literature there was for a time what seemed to be a brief stand
off between himself and what had happened within the bright
rather sudden revival of ancient metres which had formerly rather
dragged on for some decades. He had foreseen their demise, but
with others had sensed about 1965 that what seemed to them up
to then a completed victory for Modernism and Experiment and

Adventure, of which he himself had been a part, was now perhaps being rejected by a rather reactionary young non-intellectual gang of conservatives. For a fairly brief while, there had been a quiet confrontation. But Cynghanedd still had more to say. It never had been just a medieval method of ordering sound, which had stuck in a time-warp. It was an analysis of the language itself. It was in itself a systematised language, that is to say a Unity or 'System of Systems' through which poets despite themselves celebrated and honoured Form in every aspect.

And Gerallt's respect for this strange phenomenon (that had unconsciously discovered itself within the Welsh language) grew as his own poetry and knowledge of the Welsh tradition itself flourished. Conscious references to a multitude of hidden points of literary significance are felt here and there in his work, Arthur, Deiniol of course amongst the Saints, the Sagas of Llywarch and Cynddylan, The Mabinogion, Trystan and Esyllt, Dafydd ap Gwilym, Glyndŵr, Goronwy Owen (who takes up a complete poem), J. Glyn Davies and a number of contemporaries – Waldo (with two poems) and something of a soul-mate, Alun Llywelyn-Williams. We are here driving through the Welsh countryside; and as we go along we come upon numerous outcrops of the hidden Wales.

In other words, some readers of Gerallt's poems in English could find themselves lighting upon a new civilisation, richer, in so far as it recognises some of the invisible layers of life. His gentle temperament, the leisurely pace of his rhythms for the most part, and his sophisticated praise of humane standards, these all convey or explain a few sentences from an Obituary in the *Observer* at the time of his death: 'He was an extremist for moderation . . . He defended rural values by an unfearing cosmopolitanism . . . His internationalism and genuine and practical concern for the well-being and flourishing of far-flung peoples brought to his vision of his own country an extrovert sanity'.

Every, translation is of course a creative act, and produces a new poem. One of the advantages, however, an author possesses – and authority – in translating his own work is that he is free to convey in a different tongue and context exactly what he would have written had it been the original. In other words, there is no need to be over-zealous about being literal. And the bilingual reader when comparing the Welsh with the English in the following poems will discover a fair scattering of 'adaptations'. They are first-hand, and deliberate, but even the forays into difference are gentle.

It would be interesting to compare these poems with those by R. S. Thomas, who had been inspired by the same people. R. S. seems to be writing always, not so much about himself, as about an image he wants to project of himself. In Gerallt's portraits, the self is hidden, and the poet finds in the 'ordinary' person someone who is in himself or herself intensely interesting, someone who enriches our consciousness. Take the portraits of hospital patients. Although the way he 'says it' is so central here, that is concealed and we become entranced by the object itself. These are real people, not simply images to be used to vent our anger or even joy. The poet loses himself in them, whilst at the same time maintaining something of the beauty of language.

Those non-Welsh readers who may have come across Gerallt formerly, would probably have found him in anthologies; and this in his case would have been completely misleading. He has to be taken in extensio. His strength – or one of his strengths – is the charm of his character that has to be encountered over the spectrum of a fair number of poems and within a multiplicity of themes.

Occasionally, the relationship between the two languages is even more daring. Take 'Cytiau'r Gwyddelod' (Hillfort in Llŷn), 60 lines in the original, 25 in the second language. It really seems that here Gerallt, although using, even clinging to, the original, has been inspired by it to work through a new poem. He doesn't do this consistently, but does so occasionally. And the same cavalier spirit pops up everywhere, but very effectively; and certainly true to the spirit of the law, and therefore justifiable, certainly one of the right ways of translating.

I believe one of the most exciting of Gerallt's poems, 'Bellach y Barcud', (At Uwchmynydd), raises quite a new question. Because of these two versions, I suggest that we have to think now of translation as a process, in quite a different way. Gerallt, first of all, has worked from his 'Source', as we may call it, his image or vision or inspiration, and has written a Welsh poem. I believe this poem to be one of Gerallt's finest moments; what 'Mair Fadlen' was to Saunders Lewis, or 'Mewn Dau Gae' to Waldo, that too is this Hawk 'At Uwchmynydd' for Gerallt. But what he seems to have done is this. He is first provoked by the Welsh poem, then he returns to the Source and produces quite a new poem in English. The new poem is very very similar, of course, but absolutely a new poem. Still the hawk hovers, still it threatens, still it remains mysterious above the ordinary practices of day-to-day life: but –

> Are there now paths old lions have not trod
> to stumble on again? And knowing them,
> to know the eternal sanity of the sea
> and feel the aspen's tense acceptance of decay?
> In a clear sky, darkening all, the red hawk hovers.

Perhaps English readers will think of Ted Hughes in this context; but Gerallt's whole ouevre leads us to consider a completely different attitude to nature, human relationships, and identity. Indeed, we need to think more of Eliot's influence perhaps, particularly in:

> Or streets led to smoke-filled rooms at evening,
> Or we lay on beaches windswept.

Or later in the Welsh version:

> yn taenu erom, ennyd dros ddadlau,
> ryfedd ddistawrwydd, a'n puro ninnau

which leads us beyond conflict and division towards serenity and purity. And strangely this is what the hawk is about – beyond its threatening,- sanity and acceptance are there, possibly, even in the hovering itself.

Gerallt's, work deserves serious study and close experiential analysis. His later poems convince me that this present volume, which includes a number of post *Collected Poems*, that is to say post-1989, the Geese at Gregynog, and others will be something of a revelation to Welsh and non-Welsh readers alike. These lead us back even to re-consider completely Gerallt's earlier work, and his careful development. If we do that carefully, we will realise that his verse was amongst the most poignant written in Wales in the second half of the last century. Of all Welsh poets, Waldo was his predecessor. 'Cynhebrwng yn Llŷn' reminds one – though so very different in subject – of Waldo's meditation in 'Cwmwl Haf'. As we have seen, he wrote two poems in praise of Waldo. And something of the elder poet's spirit was passed on to the other.

'Shetland' is another poem of the same ilk. This again follows the same methodology of re-creation in Source Translation. The first stanza may remind an English reader of Hopkins. But Gerallt here is simply writing within the same tradition of 'sangiad' and rhythm and 'cynghanedd' that Hopkins picked up in the Vale of Clwyd. Cynghanedd has, as a prosodic language, proved itself at the end of twentieth century Wales a valuable instrument for Modernity. 'Sangiad' itself is an ancient Welsh figure. Take the first stanza of 'Petra, Georgia' where the sentence structure takes a leap. Or rather, by interference in the syntax, the verbal clause is held back 'led us', by phrases or clauses, and creates a feeling of tension and expectancy, before being resolved 'to Petra in the rain'.

In receiving an invitation to write this introduction I was honoured by Sŵ, Gerallt's widow, who was the subject of a number of the gentle love-poems in this volume. But I had already been honoured in knowing Gerallt himself, and treasure many memories of his company. At one period, we shared a room together, as fellow lecturers in the University. Both young and wild, I remember a summer evening with him scrambling a gorse-hill overlooking Aberystwyth, chatting about poetry and the future. Later, middle-aged, married, and sober, if that adjective is appropriate considering the company, I remember the two of us entertaining Hugh McDiarmid to dinner, again in Aberystwyth, and relating tales about Saunders Lewis. Now, in this volume I am honoured again by him in hearing again his powerful voice and enjoying his extraordinary but quiet company. And I know now that I will be joined by others in this remarkable pleasure.

BOBI JONES

The Problems of Translation

We may begin from the simple standpoint that poetry, by definition, being a fusion of sound and sense and an attempt to encapsulate experience within the structures and sound patterns of one particular language, cannot be translated. That is, of course, true. The translator of poetry faces a special difficulty that does not face the translator of prose. If he/she does what the translator of prose should aim to do, namely to render as precisely as possibly the literal meaning of what is being conveyed in one language into words of another, then that rendering is likely to be less than adequate. The translator's attention to meaning as conveyed to the intellect may involve a major lack of attention to some of the most important aspects of poetry – namely the different kind of meaning conveyed by rhythm and verbal music.

Each language possesses its own natural rhythms and its own verbal music and if some at least of this is to be conveyed in another language, then a compromise will almost certainly have to be arrived at in terms of the dictionary definitions of the actual words used. Furthermore, translation between languages as distinct from each other in their rhythms and sound patterns as Welsh and English are, compounds the problem. I would imagine that translation from Italian into Spanish might not be too difficult in comparison, or indeed from Welsh into Italian or Spanish. They are all languages rich in feminine endings and feminine rhymes, and all are heavily impregnated with Latin. There is little in common between the music of modern English and the music of modern Welsh. (It would be different if one were translating in Chaucer's time, but modern 'standard' English has, for example, lost most of its vowel sounds!)

Nor is that all. In addition to problems which are specifically linguistic, the translator also faces difficulties which might be more properly thought of as sociological. The social and intellectual climate of the Welsh-speaking hinterland, even today, is substantially different from that which the English-language poet relates to in the heartlands of Engl. Lit., from the accepted mid-Atlantic norms of London literary magazines and 'The Late Show'. It is not easy to specify, but it seems still possible and valid to make the kind of direct, explicit statement in a Welsh poem that would no longer be regarded as valid in a conventional English poem. I can imagine that an African poet would have similar problems, or even a poet writing out of the Deep South. In other words, it may sometimes seem necessary, when translating, not only to change the words of the poem but to change its stance as well.

In essence, an effective translator of poetry always writes what is to some degree a new poem. That being the case, however, if a translation is to be any kind of representation of another poetic experience rather than something entirely new, then it must relate reasonably closely to the form and nature of the original; it cannot simply use the original as a springboard for another poem.

And thereby lies, in my experience, having translated other people's poems as well as my own, a strong argument for a poet not translating his/her own poems at all. I find that there is a constant temptation, when rendering one's own work into another language, to refashion or rephrase what, as Eliot said, was not very well phrased in the first place, if only because one is naturally reluctant to spend time making the same poem in the same way twice. Someone else at least comes to the task with a degree of objectivity, and bases the work of translation on a text rather than on a text plus a remembered experience.

I must confess therefore that, in some cases, the translations which appear here are 'versions' rather than true translations, simply because I do not think that a straightforward 'translation' would render the Welsh experience in English with any degree of faithfulness to the original. Another poem, similar but different, seemed to be the only thing that would come close to doing it.

In specific terms, I found the business of choosing which poems to translate both difficult and frustrating. The simple problem was that those poems I most wished to translate were, in many instances, those I was least able to translate. They were the ones most bound into the fabric of the language in which they were originally written, either because of obvious devices like rhymes and internal rhymes and half-rhymes or because of subtler aspects of language like speech rhythms or even because of stances which I could neither keep nor change. Those I chose to render in the end were those whose 'message' was most straightforward and therefore those which, in some senses, were least poetic. (I am fortunate that I do not write in 'cynghanedd'; if I did, I'm certain that the extent of the loss would prevent my undertaking the task of translation at all.)

Nevertheless, for all that, for those of us who write in languages accessibly only to a few, translation, however inadequate, is the only way we have of reaching a wider audience; and reaching a wider audience is, in my view, important. Poetry, if it has any validity, expresses aspects of human experience which have in them some elements of universality. If one wishes to communicate such experience at all, there is no reason why one should wish to limit that communication to those who happen to speak the same language. I therefore welcome, with however many reservations, the huge increase in the translation of verse, and in the publication of the translation of verse, which has taken place during recent years. We must simply swallow our frustrations, abandon our purism and get on with it. Partial communication, which is what it will always be, is ultimately far far better than no communication at all.

R. G. JONES

This article first appeared in *Modern Poetry in Translation*, No. 7, 1995.

Y CERDDI

THE POEMS

PANSIE

(cyfarch merch ddu ar stryd Aberystwyth)

Gall osgo pen, gogwydd llaw,
llyfnder ysgwydd betrus,
agor drws ar galon cenedl.

Sigl a syn ysgafnder symudiad
a gwawr sydyn gwên wen
yn dringo i lygaid,

fel y gwelir, wrth grwydro'r gwres gwyrdd
goeden poinsiana am y tro cyntaf
yn dringo i'r nef;

felly'r symud a welais ddoe yn yr haul,
y llifo glân, llyfnder mewn croen
a fu'n fudr gan waed ac yn garpiau gyhyd.

Mae hi'n torri allan i redeg yn ddiamynedd,
mae hi'n gweiddi ar yr awyr y mae'n symud trwyddi,
ei phenglog onglog yn drwm, llygaid yn wreichion,
dwylo mawr yn hofran.

Mae'n aros, pen ar un ochr yn gwylio
(mae'r pen yn garreg), cyhyrau'n dynn
ar bwys ungoes; mae'n gwenu'n anferth,
a thrwy'r clwyfau hen yng nghilfachau'r wên
mae drws yn gilagored ar galon cenedl.

PANSIE

The way a head is held, dark eyes fixed far,
can change all things.
A face turned half way,
the swing and lilt of a walk,
the slow dawn of a white smile
climbing into one girl's eyes;
and all suddenly changes.

As when driving a road the first poinsiana is seen
claiming the sky,
So she moves free in the sun,
and her movements master the eye
in the land where her fathers sweated,
her walk breaks into running impatience,
shouts at the air she moves in,
head, tempest-tossed, flings fire,
hands hover half uncertain,
and all things change.

A turned face, held up to listen,
a way of walking,
a clouded smile
make patterns change
light bursts and sight is new
in this familiar environment.

TAI DUON

Rwy'n gwybod na allaf fyth eto
foduro'n ffri yn Eifionydd fel o'r blaen,
a chofio'n ysgafn fod gwreiddiau yno yn rhywle,
fod hen, hen helyntion na wyddwn i
ynghlwm wrth fawndir y lle.
                              Cofio am enwau rhithiol
fel Cwmbran a'r Ynys, Bron Menach, Bron Hendre a'r Efail,
Bwlchderwin, Glandwyfach a'r Graig Goch.

Ni allaf fyth eto. Deuthum o hyd i'r gwreiddiau.
Maent yn clymu fin nos am fy nghof,
yn gyffyrddiad dirdynnol ag esgyrn a gwaed,
ac yn arwain o faes petryal ar lethrau'r Graig Goch.

Nid oedd fy nain at y diwedd,
yn wir, yn ddim ond llestr gwag,
heb allu i weld y blodau a garai,
nac i lefaru'r geiriau y dymunai eu dweud,
nac i godi'n wyllt, fel y mynnai wneud,
i frwsio a thwtio ei thŷ.

                              Ond pan welaf
ochrau'r Graig Goch yn drwm dan rug
mwy tanbaid ar awr y machlud
nag undim a welais erioed,
a phan feddyliaf am y bedd pridd
ar y goriwaered islaw,
nid y llestr gwag a welaf fi.

                              Ac nid yn hwnnw
y bu byw ei henaid ers llawer mis, mi wn.
Aeth erstalwm ymhell o'n hamgyffred ni,
o gyrraedd ei phlant o gwmpas ei gwely.

GRANDMOTHER

(on seeing another grave)

So, knowing this, I cannot
joyride along the lanes,
cradled by distant voices, grandma's tales,

landscape of rowan and elder,
farms and fields labelled in legend,
line-drawn between me and the evening light.

Towards the end, a walnut shell,
she rocked in her bed, brown and dry,
scooped up life's windfalls spearing me with her eye.

I watched her, pillow-propped,
exchanging acid banter
with lovers long dead.

Eventually she went, leaving grey flesh,
mouldy already, on clean white sheets,
and I wrote grey words for her tombstone.

Aeth i Bant Glas ei hun cyn i'r corff marw
a holl orymdaith cynhebrwng ddringo'r allt
i orffwys ym mynwent Tai Duon.
Gwelais hi'n syllu,
ei llygaid yn syllu i gornel ystafell,
ei synhwyrau a'i meddwl yn rhannu ymgom,
ymgom gyfrin i ni, a gymerodd ei le dibwys mewn hanes
hanner canrif ynghynt.

Ond gwelais hefyd
nosweithiau gwahanol ger y tân yn ei thŷ yn Nefyn,
y fflamau'n las, a'r eira, chwedl hithau, yn dod;
y ddau ohonom yn procio ac yn pwnio'r clapiau,
yn hel hen straeon, ac yn gwybod fod yr eira yn dod.
Rwy'n cofio sawl papur chweugain coch
a sleifiais i'm poced o'i dwylo hi, heb i'm tad
wybod, na mam, fod ei harian prin
yn prynu dim amgen na llyfr i mi.
Flynyddoedd wedyn,
rwy'n cofio'r direidi yng nghornel ei llygaid
pan fentrai i'r ardd, bob amser i'r ardd, bob amser,
cribyn neu fforch yn ei llaw, gan wybod
dyfarniad y meddyg mai cadair a chegin
oedd terfynau ei byd i fod.

Ac wrth sefyll yma,
ym mynwent Tai Duon, a chofio, wrth wylio'r pridd
nad yw'n cynnwys, wedi'r cyfan, ond llestr gwag
a fu'n llestr toredig yn hir, rwy'n teimlo
grym perthynas yn nyddu'r bröydd hyn, ei bröydd hi,
i batrwm fy neunydd am byth.
Bydd rhodio eu ffyrdd
bellach yn daith dyletswydd, a gwylio eu lliwiau
yn weithred frodorol. O'r funud hon, yr wyf finnau hefyd
yn etifedd holl wylltir a mawnog a phant
a chorsydd a meysydd caregog Eifionydd fy nain.

It was only yesterday I saw that other grave.
Four children, her brothers and sisters,
all gone in a month or two. White death stole them

and left her, at ten, the family manager.
Her father, they say, lonely, married a harsh newcomer.
Her prayers were said to a half-remembered mother.

I had thought once her eyes might remain,
dark, mischief-ridden eyes. But now they're gone too,
lost in a desperate sadness, even the eyes and all.

I DEREK WALCOTT

(wrth ddarllen ei gerddi)

Mae'n corddi;
hiraeth am yr haul
heno'n fy mhoeni.

Mae d'eiriau'n crasu'n ddu
ar bob tudalen wen.

Cluniau'n llafarganu,
culion, llyfnion,
a'r dwylo'n llipa fawr.
Palmwydd
yn plygu'n ufudd.
Hen ddynion fel mwncïod
yn gyrru yn eu cwsg
ar fulod amyneddgar
tua'r môr.
Tywod tywyll, cytiau blêr,
dail mango, dail cymesur,
dail banana, dail carpiog annifyr,
dail mawr yn crogi'n uchel.
Sawr oren, sawr pydredd melys,
sawr pysgod a'r rhwydi'n we
rhyngof a'r haul coch.

Mae'n afon,
mae'n genlli na allaf ei ddofi,
mae'n llamu
trwy'r mwrllwch mawr i'w drechu.

TO DEREK WALCOTT

(on reading his poems)

It churns;
longing for the sun
unsettles me.

Your words sear black
into every white page.

Thighs chant,
narrow, smooth,
and the hands huge and slack.
Palm trees
bend obediently.
Old men like monkeys
ride in their sleep
patient mules
towards the sea.
Dark sand, ragged shacks,
mango leaves, well-proportioned,
banana leaves, awkward ragged leaves,
great leaves dangling high,
Taste of orange, sweet taste of corruption,
taste of fish and the nets a spider's web
between me and the red sun.

It's a river
a flood that I cannot tame,
it leaps through the great gloom
and slays it.

YMWELWYR

Siglodd trwy'r ward, ei jib i fyny
a'r cynfas allan i gyd,
llong hen-ffasiwn yn hwylio, llithro'n slac
i harbwr newydd, a'i sgiff o ŵr
ar raff go dynn tu ôl.

Diawl, meddai pendics Brynsiencyn,
a'i blant yn farclod o'i gwmpas wrth f'ochor,
y blydi cwîn a'i chi:
iaith farus, meddai J.T. 'r stumog, tendia di.

Aeth y ddau, y llong a'i chwch,
ymlaen at y gwely pella',
gan ddiosg het a menig, cap a bag,
cyn angori, un o bobtu'r cwilt.

Syllodd y naill a'r llall ar y pentwr cnawd,
y cynnyrch tlawd dan do'r blancedi,
gan sibrwd gair am wair a'r tywydd;
mor wlyb yw'r we'rglodd fach,
mor fain yw'r gwynt.

Ond hwn ni faliai ddim am driciau'r pridd
a'r glaw, am hen chwedloniaeth cae;
dibwys oedd popeth ond poen y golau trydan
a chric ei gefn a'r botel a'r gwely.

Daeth gosteg ar wyntoedd ei thrêd o gwmpas y ffarm,
llaciodd yr hwyliau; chwaraeodd y fam â'i wallt tenau,
ochneidiodd dros draed y gwely ar ei llipryn gŵr,
powliodd un deigryn tew i lawr ei boch.

VISITORS

She wobbled through the ward, jib raised
full canvas hoisted,
an old barque, easing slowly
into a new harbour, her skiff-husband
on a tight towrope behind.

Bugger me, said Brynsiencyn Pendix –
children an apron around his bed –
bloody Queen and her dog,
language, said JT Stomach, have a care.

The two of them, ship and skiff,
went on to the farthest bed,
disposing hat and gloves, cap and bag,
before anchoring either side of the quilt.

They stared at the pile of flesh,
a poor crop gathered in under blankets,
whispered a word of hay-bales and weather,
how the small meadow was flooded,
how cold the wind.

But he cared little for the vagaries
of soil and rain, a field's fables;
there was nothing but the glaring light,
a throbbing back, a bottle and a bed.

It was a lull for her in the trade winds
around the farm; sails slackened,
she fingered his hair, sighed at her small husband;
one fat tear crawled down her cheek.

Ac yna cipiodd yr awel drachefn;
gwisgodd ei het, rhwbiodd ei menig sbon
yn annwyl am gyrn ei llaw,
cadwynodd y tad a hwyliodd allan.

Drannoeth bu farw'r bachgen yn ei gwsg,
heb yngan gair erioed o'i le wrth ferch,
heb garu neb ond gwynt yr eithin du.

Aeth hithau'r fam i'r iard i fwydo'r ieir.

Then she took the breeze once more,
put on her hat, smoothed brand-new gloves
carefully over hard knuckles,
roped in the father and sailed out.

In a day or two the lad died in his sleep
without ever baring his heart to a girl,
his love reserved for the wind in the gorse
and the mother went into the yard to feed the hens.

Y GWRANDAWR

O gylch yr ysbyty, ef oedd y gwrandäwr.
Safai'n bren, fore a hwyr, uwchben sawl cwyn
am yr ail a'r trydydd a'r pedwerydd tro,
a'i gydymdeimlad, fel afon Duw, yn llenwi'r lle.

Dyn cyffredin oedd Dic, wedi'r cyfan,
sigarét rhwng ei fysedd, rhywbeth yn bod ar ei berfedd,
ambell reg yn blaguro'n wyllt
yng ngerddi trefnus ei frawddegau prin.

Gartref yn Nefyn, ni fentrai'r tu hwnt i ystrydeb.
Âi gyda'i feic bob bore i'w weithdy saer,
linc-mi-lonc, gan anwybyddu'r byd.
Codai ei het, bid sicr, i ferched y pentref,
a gwenai mewn parch i gonfensiwn.
Ond ni fentrai geisio adnabod neb.

Trwy'r dydd, byddai'n trin ei goed,
fel pe bai'r coed yn fwy byw na dynion,
ac ar ddiwedd y busnes, yntau'n ofalus bob amser
i orffen ei waith, gosodai ei gap am ei ben,
gan wthio'r beic bustachlyd i'r stryd lawn pobl,
a chyrchu tuag adref yn nhywyllwch ei enaid ei hun.

Twrch daear o ddyn oedd Dic. Ond yma daeth golau i'w fyd.
Nis ganed ef i adrodd straeon doniol wrth y plant,
a chadw pen-rheswm ar bwyllgor lleol a ledio emyn.
A phan ddaeth i gyntedd angau, i'r llonydd gwyn
tragywydd sy'n fywyd dros dro mewn ysbyty,
gwelodd mai gwrando oedd ei waith. Daeth golau i'w fyd.

THE LISTENER

Around the hospital, he was the listener.
He would stand, a tree, morning and evening, above many
  a groan
for the second and the third and the fourth time,
his compassion, like God's river, filling the room.

A commonplace man was Dic, after all,
a cigarette between his fingers, something in his guts,
an occasional curse sprouting wildly
in the tidy gardens of his rare sentences.

Home in Nefyn, he'd not venture beyond a cliché.
He'd go on his bike each morning to his carpenter shop,
dilly-dally, ignoring the world.
He'd raise his hat, to be sure, to the village girls,
and smile in deference to convention.
But he'd not venture to try to know anyone.

Through the day, he'd handle his wood
as if the wood were more alive than men,
and at the end of business, always careful
to complete his work, he'd put his cap on his head,
push the bungling bike to the street full of people,
and make for home in the dark of his own soul.

A mole of a man was Dic. But here light came to his world.
He was not born to tell funny stories to children,
keep a cool head on a local committee, lead a hymn.
And when he came to death's forecourt, to the white eternal
quiet that is life for a time in hospital,
he saw that his work was to listen. Light came to his world.

Aeth o wely i wely, mor surbwch fud ag erioed,
gyda'i stwmp sigarét yn thuser gweddi
a chymerodd i'w god holl boenau'r uffern honno,
y gwayw sy'n argoel marwolaeth i'r sawl a'i gŵyr,
a llethdod y gorwedd maith.

                    Pan ddeuai'r nos
dychwelai i'w wely ei hun a'i glustiau'n agored,
yn gyfrwng cymundeb rhyngddo a'r byd.

Ef oedd y gwrandäwr a gludai'n beichiau ni
fesul un ac un i ryw domen yn rhywle,
fel y cluda'r môr ei gargo i ebargofiant.

He went from bed to bed, sullenly mute as ever,
with his cigarette stump a censer of prayer
and took to his sack all the pangs of that hell,
the pain that's a portent of death to those who know it,
and the languor of lying so long.

                       When night would come,
he'd go back to his own bed, his ears open,
a means of communion between himself and the world.

He was the listener who'd bear our burdens
one by one to some dungheap somewhere,
as the sea bears its cargo to oblivion.

I EWAN MacLACHLAN

(Saif cofeb i fardd Gaelaidd mewn mynwent yn Fort William.
Claddwyd ef, yn ôl yr arysgrif Saesneg a Gaeleg, yn ardal
wledig Ardgour.)

Ewan Maclachlan, mae'r bompren eiddil
rhyngom a'th hiraeth di wedi hen bydru.
Nid Eóbhan oedd Ewan, hyd yn oed
yn y Gymraeg, gan y sawl sy'n ei medru.

Est yn ôl, medd y gair, i Ardgour.
Ond a oes a erys o'r dras farddonol
yn Ardgour, neu yma yn ninas Duncan
neu yn unman? Mae'r llwyth brodorol?

Islaw eisteddai merch ar garreg fedd
gyda chyfrol o gerddi; hi a minnau a'i chi
yn y fynwent wag a'r chwyn yn teyrnasu.
Darllen'sai gerddi, ond nid, Eóbhan, dy gerddi di.

A glywsai hi fod dy lwch a llwch gwareiddiad
yn gorwedd draw yn Ardgour di-goed,
a mudandod gwacterau yn gwylio drosto?
Naddo. Dim gair. Dim sôn amdanat erioed.

Nid rhyngom ni a thi – Gymry'r adladd
a'r Gael – y mae'r bwlch di-bont, ond rhwng heddiw
a phob doe cymdogol, rhwng y cyfnos
niwclear a gwawr pob symlrwydd gwiw.

Erys iaith, erys murddun ar dir, erys ysbryd
Eóbhan Maclachlan dy daid, MacDonnell o Keppoch,
ardderchog yn eu clwyfau ar Culloden,
erys machlud Ardgour yn glwyfus, nosweithiol goch.

FOR EWAN MacLACHLAN

(A memorial to a Gaelic poet stands in a graveyard in
Fort William. He was buried, according to the inscription
in English and Gaelic, in Ardgour.)

Ewan MacLachlan, the ricketty footbridge
between us and your singing is long down;
it's Ewan now, not Eobhan, even in Welsh
for the remnant who speak it.

You lie, so it says, in Ardgour.
But what is left now that is yours
in Ardgour, or here in Duncan's town
or anywhere? Where are the poet's songs?

Nearby a girl sits on a tombstone
reading verse; she and her dog and I
own the tipsy graveyard, thighdeep, thistled.
She reads verse, but Eobhan, not yours.

Has she heard that your bones and the bones
of all civilized living lie in treeless Ardgour,
watched by the sentry hillsides? No.
Not a word. Not a grieving word ever.

The chasm yawns uncrossed, not between us
so much, the Welsh, and the Gael,
but between this grey tomb and every yesterday,
between this dark afternoon and mornings of simpler light.

Words, words remain; ruins of houses squat on Mull;
ghosts of Eobhan Maclachlan, your father's father
and MacDonnell of Keppoch, fierce at Culloden,
walk where each sunset weeps on Ardgour, nightly raw and red.

CERDD I'R HEN DYDDYNNWR

(neu'n fwy manwl, i bwy bynnag a gododd ei dŷ yng
nghysgod Banc Llety Ifan Hen yng Ngogledd Ceredigion)

'Dydw i ddim o'r farn,
a goleddir ymysg beirdd a berchir
gan Gymry ysgolheigaidd a dinesig
yn y *Reform Club*, heb sôn am gymdeithasau
gwerthfawrogi barddoniaeth mewn prifysgolion
yn Rhydychen, Ibadan a Tennessee,
mai twpsyn oeddit.

Deuthum ar ddiwrnod sidan ym Medi
dros y silff o lwybr
at Fanc Llety Ifan Hen, a gwelais
i lawr yn y pant,
gwmpas dy ddealltwriaeth.

Rhwng yr ochrau coch, caregog,
dau gae yn las gan ofal,
a channllath oddi wrthynt, heibio i'r mwyn marw,
perth glòs yn cynhesu dy dŷ,
coed gellyg ac afalau ac un geiriosen,
y nant wedi'i phontio
a'i dŵr yn bistyll sy'n glir
ymhob rhyw dywydd.

A phan gerddais ymlaen
a'r gaeaf yn biws am bump o'r gloch,
heibio i Graigypistyll hyd at Lannerch-clwydau,
roedd y meini anferth
a dreiglwyd rywbryd i Benycastell
yn gymdogion llonydd dros y ffens;
hwythau unwaith yn dai annedd, neu'n demlau
i ryw gredo y tu hwnt i ddirnad gwareiddiad
sy'n parchu pridd yn ôl trwch ei gemegau.

TO THE OLD HILL-FARMER

(whomsoever he may be, who built his house in the shadow
of Banc Llety Ifan Hen, north Ceredigion)

I'm not of the opinion – popular though that may be
among poets well thought of
by scholarly, urbane Welshmen
in the *Reform Club*, not to mention societies
for the appreciation of poetry in the Universities
of Oxford, Ibadan and Tennessee
that you were a numbskull.

I came in a silky day in September
over that shelving path
to Banc Llety Ifan Hen, and I saw,
down in the hollow,
the extent of your understanding.

Between the red, stony hillsides,
two fields green with care
and a hundred yards away – past the dead mine –
a tight hedgerow warming your house,
pear-trees and apple-trees and one cherry-tree,
the brook neatly bridged
and its water clear
in all weathers.

And as I walked on,
with the winter at my shadow at five o'clock,
past Craigpistyll to Llannerch-clwydau,
the great stones
that were dragged once to Penycastell
were silent neighbours breasting the ridge;
they, too, had once been dwelling-places, or temples
raised to a religion beyond the grasp of men
who rate the richness of earth by its chemical components.

Dros Foel y Golomen, roedd siafftiau'r haul yn siffrwd,
er, mae'n wir, mai cipolwg yn unig
a fentrai drosodd i wastadedd y ddau gae glas.

Yng ngarwedd y mynydd, a'r gwynt
yn ddychryn i'r gannwyll,
o ble daeth y cynhesrwydd a barodd
i ti osod un geiriosen
ymysg caledi'r eirin tagu?

Yma, fel yn Rwsia Tolstoi a Siecoff,
fel mewn tlws berllannau hen wareiddiadau pell,
roedd blodau'r ceirios, a'r gellyg wedyn a'r afalau,
yn ernes flynyddol o ledneisrwydd nas profid
fel arall.
A lledneisrwydd yw hanfod bywyd gwâr.
        'Dydw i ddim o'r farn
        mai twpsyn oeddit.

Over Moel y Golomen
the sun's final shafts filtered,
although it's true that only a glimmer
ventured over to the hollow and its two green fields.

On that harsh mountain, where the wind
terrorised your candle,
where did you find the inner warmth
that made you plant a cherry-tree
among those tough and bitter sloes?

Here, as in the Russia of Tolstoy and Chekov,
as in the sweet orchards of distant civilisations,
the cherry-blossom, and then the pears, and the apples,
were a proof, every year, of a grace that was otherwise absent
and grace is the touchstone of civilised living.
I am not of the opinion
that you were a numbskull.

OFFEIRIAD GWLAD

Eisteddai yn ei gadair
a'i ben llew yn llonydd
a'i lygaid ymhell.

Eisteddai yn y tŷ mawr hwnnw
yn yr ystafell wag
a'r te'n oer yn y cwpan
ac arswyd ei swydd amdano.

Eisteddai'r oriau hir yn ei gadair,
wedi i'r brain glwydo,
a'i lygaid yn gwrando,
ond ni ddaeth un llais i'w gysuro
na thaw ar y mudandod mawr.

COUNTRY PARSON

He sat in his chair

his lion head still
his eyes distant

He sat in that vast house
in the empty room
the tea cold in its cup
his awful calling wrapped around him

He sat long hours in his chair
after the crows had slept
his eyes listening
but no voice came to comfort him
nor any end to the great silence

LLWYBR YR AFON

Mae'r llwybr wedi tyfu'n gyfarwydd,
Pob tro ac anwastadrwydd,
Pob deilen, mewn ffordd o siarad,
Yn mesur acen a churiad
Fy nhaith. Taith fer o ruthr y dŵr
Dan bont y pentref, yn ôl i'r merddwr
Llathraidd dywyll dan y coed crwm.
Ond ynddi mae siâp fy mydysawd
Erbyn hyn yn gwisgo gïau a chnawd.
Rhwng y brigau, yn y gogledd, Ursa Major,
Heuliau tân, pontydd goleuni, yn agor
Drysau, coridorau'n ôl i Sycharth, Abermenai, i bell
Gywyddau gaeaf yn neuaddau'r castell,
Llewyrch bregus y torchau, a'r fflamau'n wres;
Fel y ffrwydrodd seren Bethlehem unwaith hefyd ei neges
Anhygoel, o bellter llaid ac anrhefn y cynfyd anwar.
A'r brigau eu hunain, maent hwythau'n fyd gwâr,
Yn fap dianwadal, yn dŷ
Diadfail. Maent yn bwrpas. Mae'r llu
Diamser yn warant perthynas i minnau.
Ond wedyn, heibio i'r pwll dyfnaf, ar graig, gynnau,
Gwelais ddau lonydd, annisgwyl yn syllu, nid ar y disglair sêr
Ond ar feidrol gnawd, a'r gannwyll wêr,
Fel gynt i'r bardd, yn ddewisach cwmni,
Pa mor farwol bynnag, na'r sêr dirifedi.

THE RIVERSIDE PATH

The path has become familiar,
Each turn and each flaw in its surface,
Each leaf, in a manner of speaking,
Measures the beat and bearing
Of my journey. A brief journey from the rush
Of waters beneath the bridge to the dark
Still pools under the bowed trees.
But in it the shape of my cosmos
By now wears sinew and flesh.
Between the branches northwards, Ursa Major,
Suns of fire, bridges of light, opens
Doors, corridors back to Sycharth, Abermenai,
To distant winter odes in castle halls,
To flickering torchlight and warm fires;
How the star of Bethlehem once too exploded
Its incredible message to primitive chaos.
And the branches themselves, they're a civilised world,
A map that's not unreliable, a house that's not
Ruined. They are a purpose. That host beyond time
Guarantees my own belonging. But then,
Beyond the deepest pool, on a rock, just now,
I saw two still figures unaware, staring,
Not at bright stars but at mortal flesh,
And one worn candle, as it once did to the poet,
Became more desirable, however mortal,
Than the light of innumerable stars.

CYTIAU'R GWYDDELOD

(sef y gaer fynyddig ar Garnfadrun yn Llŷn)

'Dianwyd ydyw'r dynion'
a gododd gaer ar y graig hon.
I minnau, ar wifrau'r nerfau,
parablant eiriau na ellir mo'u rhestru
yng ngeiriaduron gwybod
ond sy'n atsain o hyd ac o hyd
yn y dyfnjiwn, yn selerydd bod.

Gwreichion ar eingion a chloncian
a chlecian carnau
yng ngwyll coch yr ogof garreg.
Robert Jones y gof, a'i fwstas ffasiynol,
yn ddiferol-gyhyrog wrth ei fegin;
llifodd eu hystyfnigrwydd hedegog,
eu dychymyg tywyll, trwy ei waed yntau;
yntau a'r hen geffylau llonydd,
a'u stêm a'u ffroeni sydyn,
erbyn hyn i gyd yn esgyrn gwyn
dan y gors laith yn Eifionydd.

A bu morthwylio arall ar graig yn Arfon,
llwch llwyd yn glasu gwythïen
ar gefn llaw, yn wyn ar aeliau,
yn llifo'n frwnt trwy les yr ysgyfaint,
a'r cyrff cam yn y sgidiau mawr
yn rhygnu'u ffordd yn y bore bach
o beswch i beswch tra parai anadl.

A bu rhain ymorwst â'r gelyn
perffeithaf i gyd, y gwynt sy'n malu'r tonnau
gefn nos y tu hwnt i'r bae –
mor fregus eu hanadl gynnes yn erbyn y gwynt.

HILLFORT IN LLŶN

They built for a day's respite, hardly more,
but from limestone lairs, moss bound now,
voices echo in the mind's dungeon.

Anvil sparks, clatter of hooves in a sunset smithy,
my grandfather, moustache akimbo, dew-sprayed with sweat;
their rhythms beat through his capillaries.

Hammered too on rocks in Arfon. Grey dust in blue veins,
grey-white in young eyes, cut clumsy through lungs' lace.
Bent youth in borrowed boots dragged their thin legs,
cough by cough, through each damp winter. Their people too.

All this took place within time's ordinance.
And later the waiting on mean earth,
coaxing mud-fettered fields of November,
watching the slow churning in dairies where ice formed
  on slates
in festive December.

Ac yna, o'r diwedd, bu disgwyl maith yr holl amaethu,
y dofi a fu ar ymchwydd ifanc y creu
dros rostir lle y mae garwedd y ddraenen ddu
yn esgor bob gwanwyn
ar raeadrau'r blodau gwyn,
ar wylltineb, goruchafiaeth, gorfoledd ergydiol powld
   y blodau gwyn.

Yn eu pryd y digwyddodd y pethau hyn
ac yn nhrefn amser,
oherwydd y dygnu a'r dal ati a fu
yn y llaid ar y cowt yn Nhachwedd
ac yn oerni'r aelwydydd cerrig, ac yn y llaethdy
lle y mae'r rhew yn haen ar lechen fore Nadolig.

Ond nid y fro werdd rhwng y gaer lwyd a'r môr oedd ffrâm
   eu cyfanfyd.
O fewn y penglogau hirion, y tu hwnt i'r llygaid tywyll,
roedd y rhain yn clwydo yn y nos
ar ymyl rhyw fôr goleuni,
a hwnnw'n tyneru rhychau'r tymhorau
ar eu hwynebau hwy.

Nid yw'r cnawd ond gwellt,
ond o'r eglwysi bach mewn llwyni,
a'r trydan yn gynnwrf parhaus ynddynt o hyd,
edrychent, fy mhobl i, allan trwy'r gwydrau plwm
heibio i'r Crist crog,
heibio i'r mynydd cyfarwydd
i'r lle y mae sail rhyw wybod anghyffwrdd.

Ac mae rhyw fodau fu unwaith yn llunio –
'Gwŷr trymion uwch gwar trimor' –
lochesau rhag min gwynt Ionor
yn cydio'n dynn yn yr hyn wyf finnau;
'Dwys mudion gwŷr dis'mudiad'
yn estyn dwylo trwy'r grug o fore'r cread.

Such realist landscapes, oak-framed,
do not contain them. Inside long skulls,
seated by leaded windows in dark churches,
their shores were touched by a sea of light,
its waters easing away the seasons' hardships.

And now those ancient men who once built here
laborious shelter from the world's winds
look down with holy pity from their high ruin
at the weeping wall we have all come to
through long and desert journeys of the mind.

BELLACH Y BARCUD

(i fardd o Sais)

Bellach y barcud a ganfu bob llwybr.
Dan gynfas yr wybr nid erys llecyn
yn gudd rhag ei lygaid gwydr.
Mae gwaed ei grafangau ar lethrau'r rhedyn,
ac nid oes aderyn na chenfydd gysgod
sydyn, ofnadwy, terfynol ei ddyfod.

Pa fodd y mae cyrraedd unigedd heno?
A'r drain yn dringo eu diogi dros lwyni
pob prydferth; pob clust a gais wrando
yn llawn bloedd, yn llawn cri penwynni.
Inni a erys, beirianwyr gwallgof-fyd,
unrhyw osteg rhag llygaid y barcud?

Gwyddost ganwaith ar lawer awr trafod
i ni ei goncro, a chanfod hedd rhyngom;
ger mor Mehefin ei ganfod,
neu'n nerth gyda'r nos yn disgyn arnom,
yn taenu erom, ennyd dros ddadlau,
ryfedd ddistawrwydd, a'n puro ninnau.

A rhyfedd i ni ein dau ei ddenu,
rhyfedd fod rhannu yn rhinwedd unigedd.
Rhyfeddach fod amser wedi cymylu,
ninnau mor aml mewn amryfusedd
yn gwawdio ei fawredd, cymod
a wybu unwaith ei graidd a'i hanfod.

Os erys llwybr na cherddodd hen lew,
diau y cawn ei adnabod eto;
ei adnabod sydd raid, sydd raid, os glew
a fyddwn i dreiddio, i ddarganfod bro
a brodyr, gwraidd eu bod. Ond och, difywyd
yr ysbryd heno dan lygaid rhyfelgoch y barcud.

AT UWCHMYNYDD

(on meeting an old college friend)

No path the hawk can't spy,
no seemly walk that's hidden
from his eye. Blood spilt by him
stains heather even here. Birds all around,
fear-shrill, trill out his coming.

Strong briars choke, claw, bite
in this calm place. (Perched
on our nightmare footplate, careering on,
we lunge for the brake) Cold hawk
above looks down and bides his time.

Times, momentary pauses in time's passing,
once let us find winding paths
to a June sea, gulls at anchor,
or streets led to smoke-filled rooms at evening,
or we lay on beaches windswept in summer.

Are there now paths old lions have not trod?
To stumble on again? And knowing them,
to know the eternal sanity of the sea
and feel the aspen's tense acceptance of decay?
In a clear sky, darkening all, the red hawk hovers.

CYNHEBRWNG YN LLÝN

O gopa'r Garn
gwelid patrwm.

Caeau bychain, gwrychoedd eithin,
cwilt daearyddol taclus
a ffridd y rhedyn a'r llus
yn cydoddef, er yn anfoddog,
y cynllwyn.

Ac felly gyda'n cymdeithas.
Patrymog oedd pob perthynas,
ffrwyth blynyddoedd bwygilydd
o docio gofalus a chloddio a chau,
o wybod lled pob adwy,
o wybod, fel yr oedd angen,
pryd i gloi'r llidiart.

Yna fe ddaeth angau,
hen losgfynydd daearyddiaeth dyn.
Ni allwn ond gwylio'i lafa'n dylifo,
ei gyntefigrwydd di-siâp yn treiddio,
gwrychoedd gwâr ar chwâl
a phopeth yn finiog, yn gorneli
heddiw fel yr oedd ar y dechrau,
cyn dyfod trefn.

Safwn wedyn yn noeth
gan syllu'n wyllt ar ein gilydd;
dim gatiau i'w cau,
tir y naill yng nghaeau'r llall
gan mor ddigyfaddawd y môr
diddethol a lifodd i mewn.

FUNERAL IN LLŶN

From the crest of the Cairn
one saw a pattern.

Small fields, hedges of gorse,
a tidy geographic quilt
and a sheep-walk of fern and whinberries
enduring together, though reluctantly,
the scheme.

And so with our society.
Each relationship was patterned,
the fruit of years joined end to end
of careful pruning and digging and enclosing,
of knowing the width of each gap,
of knowing, as there was need,
when to lock the gate.

Then death came,
the old volcano in man's geography.
We can only watch its lava flowing,
its shapeless primitiveness penetrating,
cultivated hedges scattered
and everything clear-edged, cornered
today as it was in the beginning,
before the coming of order.

We stand afterwards naked
staring wildly at each other;
no gates to be shut,
one's land in another's fields,
so uncompromising the indiscriminate
sea that flowed within.

Yfory, ailadeiledir y gwrychoedd,
cau'r bylchau
a thrennydd daw patrwm newydd
diogel;
cerddwn yn weddus trwy'r adwy briodol.
ond heddiw ffrwydrodd llosgfynydd
ac edrychwn
          ym myw llygaid ein gilydd
yn noeth.

Tomorrow, the hedges will be rebuilt,
the breaks closed
and two days hence will come a new safe
pattern;
we will walk decorously through the proper gap.
But today a volcano erupted
and we look
            deep into each other's eyes
naked.

BALŴN LAS – UWCH Y SGWÂR COCH

Balŵn las fore Sul uwch y Sgwâr coch,
uwch y gaer goch a'i baner nad yw'n goch
bellach ond un o'i lliwiau; mae'n codi,
troelli uwch y maes awyr, mae'n cylchu
yn anadl y dydd uwch adladd hanes.

Nid wedi'i cholli y mae'r hogyn
ond wedi llacio gafael ar y llinyn
yn araf fwriadus, a'i gollwng yn rhydd,
ei glas i'r glas; saif yntau'n llonydd,
coesau cloff ar led, llygaid yn astud.

Gerllaw, mewn siwtiau Sul, aros y mae'r werin,
nid am chwyldro, nid am wyrth gan Yeltsin,
dim ond am gipolwg, mewn bedd sy ar agor,
ar wyneb gwêr yn y gwyll marmor –
gwobr wanwynol ddigon derbyniol i'r plant.

Ond iddo ef, nid oes unpeth yn y cread crwn
ond y smotyn glas yn pellhau; i hwn,
fel i bâr a ynysir ar gyfandir cariad,
mae'r byd yn gyflawn yng ngofod un eiliad,
mae ef a'r gell a ollyngodd yn anwahanod.

Dilyna, ei freichiau ar led, gan faddau
simsanrwydd ei briciau o goesau,
ehediad yr aderyn a greodd,
heb weld daearolion sy'n cilio o'i ffordd,
na'r wên wan ar eu genau.

Mae hyn, mae'n debyg, yn rhyw fath o heddwch,
gyda'r fam welw'n gwarchod o bell, heb ofni diogelwch
y foment. (Eto mae'i llygaid hi a'i dwylo
tenau, a theneuwch brau ei chudynnau,
yn ernes o ormes hen ryfeloedd.)

A BLUE BALLOON OVER RED SQUARE

Sunday morning; a blue balloon over Red Square,
over the red fort and its flag in which red
is no longer the one colour; it rises,
circles above that great field, swirled
by the day's breath over stubbled history.

It was not that the boy lost it,
released it rather, let go the string
deliberately, slowly, and set it free,
blue against blue; and then stands still,
crooked legs apart, watching.

Nearby, in Sunday suits, the people wait
for no revolution, nor any Yeltsin miracle,
only for a glimpse, in an open tomb,
of a waxen face in marble gloom –
an apt enough spring treat for the children.

For him, there's nothing real in the whole world
but the dying blue dot; for him,
as for lovers marooned by love,
the cosmos is all contained within,
he and the cell he set free forever inseparable.

He pursues, arms spread wide, forgetting
the blight of his matchstick legs,
the flying bird he created,
blind to earthbound creatures stepping
from his path, a slight smile on their lips.

This, perhaps, is a kind of peace,
a pale mother watching from afar
without fear. (Yet her eyes and her thin
hands and the thin strands of her hair
speak clearly enough of wars that have been.)

Na, nid math! Nid oes mwy. Ger y llyn llwm
adref ganol gaeaf, awyr yn ddu ac eira'n drwm
ond heddwch angau yw, heddwch byd disymud,
heddwch y clo clwm, heddwch amdo.

Rhyfela yw dull y byd. Clwyfus ac ansicr,
lleol heb leoliad, fel enfys ar dir,
gwibiog fel gwynt yn y coed, yw hanfod heddwch;
os y pery'n hwy, angau yw, oerfel a maith lonyddwch,
negyddiaeth ffôl pob gwaith a phob gorffwys wedi gwaith.

To make war is the way of the world.
Local without location, like a rainbow,
elusive as wind in the trees is the nature
of peace. Should it grow more substantial
it would grow cold, cold and rigid as death.

Soon they'll walk home, past the silent church,
past the red soldiers who are also children,
leaving behind the clocktower bell's tolling,
hammer on steel, measuring out the blows
that fall, here and everywhere, on children and mothers.

JARLSHOF, SHETLAND

O'r awyr, yn yr haul, un bore wedi'i sgrwbio'n lân,
gwelais batrymau gwyrddlas, gwynlas, gwyn,
yn chwarae ar dywod lle na bu ôl troed
ond troed aderyn erioed yn llidio'r lle,
a theimlais wacter ofn.

Wrth eistedd ar fynydd Enlli, a'r hwyr hir
yn felyn ar Llŷn – y tir mawr, malltod i bob ynyswr –
mae'r canol wedi symud, mae'r hyn sy'n arferol yn wahanol.
Yma, senglrwydd pethau sy'n normal;
mae'r byd yn unau, yn unigrywiau i gyd:
un ddafad wen ddiberyg,
un wylan, a'i baruster heidiog ymron yn raslonrwydd,
un pumbys piws yn hongian yn enbyd dros y dibyn peryclaf,
ac un drych cam o gnawd a breuddwyd
yn undod cymen yma am ennyd
hyd nes y bydd rhywbeth bach yn eu nithio.
Mae Uwchmynydd, dyrnaid o dai, yn orboblog,
ac Aberdaron yn fetropolis anhyfryd.

Felly hefyd wrth sefyll ar gerrig Jarlshof,
a gweld yn fychan trwy'r ewyn rhacs
forfil deheuol Fair Isle;
mae'r cwmpawd yn cynddeiriogi, mae Gogledd yn Dde,
a'r almanac mewnol yn jymbl o ddyddiau pytiog
a thymhestloedd cyntefig.
Mae tai culion o'r cynfyd
yn cwningo i'r penrhyn, yn dywyll gan wres daear,
ac yn gofyn haul chwedloniaeth ym mol y gaeaf
i oddef y curo hir – a rhyw gof pell am yr haf.

Cerddwch fin nos ar Burra,
a'r machlud gwag yn ffyrnig aneglur dros Foula;
gyrrwch dros y corsydd eithin blêr i Unst

SHETLAND

From leaflight windblown Islander, sun-dappled,
young waves, blue-green, blue-white, white,
excite, entwine over the lonely sand.

Singularity prevails:
one herring-gull, its tribal greed
at one remove, approaches elegance;
one hopscotch trace of bird's trefoil
validates the shore's virginity.

Later, touchdown achieved, galetorn on Jarlshof,
the centre shifts, norms are abnormal;
whaleback, spraywracked, Fair Isle lies southerly,
compass unhinged, North's South, mind's almanac tipsy.
Viking burrows pockmark the headland, wringing out
earth's warmth, suns of legend
soothe the rain's whiplash.

a syllwch ar fôr lle y mae'r llawr rhew
o fewn milltir i'r gorwel yn ystod y dyddiau du:
mae'r golau'n taro nodau
anghyfarwydd llwyd ar dannau'r ymennydd.

Nid anghysbell chwaith, ond pell-ganolog yw'r lle,
fel gydag unrhyw le sy'n drwm dan hanes.
Fel gydag ambell hen ŵr, hwylus,
mater o ddewis yw bodolaeth cymdogion iddo,
ac mae'i wyrion a'i fân gyfnitherod trefol a diwreiddiedig
yn rhy bell i feithrin perthynas. Lliw'r hunan sy'n cyfrif,
lliw'r hunan a chân môr-forynion yn galw'n barhaus
dros y cefnfor llwm o'r dyfnderoedd iâ,
a gosgorddion o dorchau tân yn Ionawr
a chychod mawr yn fflam yn erbyn y lloer
ac arwyr tywyll yn plymio o'r diwedd i'r dwfn.

Walk then at evening on Burra,
day dying furious, aflame over Foula,
cross unsheared gorse,
look seaward where the icepack gathers,
grey chords vibrate along the wires.

Survival of self is all.
Sea-maidens moan from the deep
all winter long, naked torches march,
great boats aglare, flare out against the moon,
brave embers yield at last to the cold sea's grasp.

PETRA, GEORGIA

Yng nghysgod meindwr Elbruz, a'r Caucasus eraill
o'r golwg yn y niwl o'i gwmpas, fel hyn
yn union y digwyddodd pethau.

Beirdd penwan meddw Colchis
yn pesgi'n swyddogol ar rigwm a phill
ac yn ein tywys,
wedi'r gwin a'r gwenieithu,
wedi'r sglefrio ysgafn dros wyneb dieithrwch,
yn falch i Petra yn y glaw.

I'r waliau gwlybion hyn yn Ajara
daeth Jason a'i filwyr, arwyr Groeg, dros y Môr Du,
a Heracles hwyrach, ac Orffews,
meibion Zëws, holl ragorolion bore'r byd
ar drywydd anfarwoldeb.

A thrwy hud cariad fe'i cawsant.
Neu, i fod yn fanwl gywir, trwy chwant cnawd
a meinder corff a chusanau poethion
fe gipiwyd y Cnu Aur.

Bradychodd Medea dad a gwlad er ei fwyn
a dychwelodd y goresgynwyr gwacsaw
i Roeg ac i feysydd chwedloniaeth.

Wedyn y drin: y tywallt gwaed afradlon
yng Nghorinth – Pelias, Glawce, Creon a'r plant
i gyd yn ysglyfaeth ddiangen.

A beth sydd a wnelo hyn â'n hymweliad ninnau?
Ein dringo baglog trwy'r glaw mân
gan gyfnewid ieithoedd anneall:

PETRA, GEORGIA

Heavy poets of Colchis, fisting out rhythms,
led us, after all the wassail and wooing,
after light-footed skating
over frozen lakes of estrangement,
to Petra in the rain.

To these wet walls in Ajara
came Jason, the heroes of Helles,
across the ghostly sea,
hunting immortality like a whale.

Through love they found it,
or, to be more precise,
through the lusts of the flesh
and the litheness of bodies,
the Golden Fleece was grabbed.
Medaea betrayed father and nation for it
and the cavalier conquerors
returned to Greece.

Then came disaster, prodigal
spilling of blood in Corinth,
Pelias, Glaucon, Creon and the children,
all bloody in death.

What then of us? Our clumsy
clambering through the rain,
exchanging codes of incomprehension,
Fridon and Jamal and Costia
and the three of us,
through the long grass and the ferns
to a pile of wet stones?

Fridon a Jamal a Costia,
Gillian a Meic a minnau,
trwy'r glaswellt a'r rhedyn gwlyb at y pentwr cerrig?
Onid y presennol hwn
y teithio gobeithiol hwn,
y ffeithiau rhyddieithol hyn,
yw'r unig wirioneddau a wyddom?

Ynteu ai'r gwir yw fod anian
Jason a Heracles a Medea'n llechu,
a thranc Pelias a Glawce a Chreon a'r plant,
nid yn y cerrig hyn,
nac mewn unrhyw bridd,
nac mewn amser,
ond y trobwll diwaelod
sy ynghudd yn ein llygaid ni a'u llygaid hwythau,
yn y cynddelwau sy'n clymu Colchis a Chatraeth ynghyd,
y ddewiniaeth gyffredin a gododd ei phen trwm
fel hen lew'n deffro yn y gwair
yn Petra yn y glaw?

Drannoeth, mewn awyren, oerodd y cof am chwedlau.
Roedd popeth yn ffaeledig sofietaidd, fel arfer,
y bwyd yn wael, y stiwardesau'n ddiras,
ac yna, uwchben y cymylau,
yn ynys ar ynys ar ynys i'r pellter,
cododd y Caucasus anhygoel eu pennau.

Are these prosaic facts
not the only truth we know?
Or is it the truth that frissons
of Jason and Medaea lurk,
and the fate of Pelias and Creon and the children,
not in these stones
but in the bottomless whirlpool
that spins in our eyes and theirs,
the common witchcraft that raises its eyes
like an old lion waking up in the grass.

Next day, warm in an aircraft, legends faded;
all was fallible, as ever,
the food coarse, the stewardesses perfunctory,
until above the clouds,
island upon island into the distance,
the peaks of the Caucasus thrust up their white heads.

MENEZ HOM

Ar Menez Hom, gwelais, a daeth sgrech i'm llygaid,
dun olew rhidyllog gan fwledi
yn rhythu allan o'r bwlch yn y concrit tyllog.

Ar Menez Hom, nad yw'n haeddu enw mynydd,
safodd amser yn llonydd.
Roedd y grug a'r banadl yn ymwthio'n dymhorol
trwy olion carpiog y rhyfel diweddaraf,
a'r adar yn codi o'r coed islaw
ac yn mynnu hedfan heibio
i'r lle llonydd nad yw'n fynydd.

Roedd caniad ehedydd yn binacl;
y ddau ehedydd, gan mor isel y tir,
yn dringo'n uwch i'r glas grisial,
a'u trydar yn rhithlen gynlluniedig
dros y grug a'r banadl y diwrnod hwnnw.

Ar y cyntaf o Fedi, 1944, roedd niwl hydref
eisoes yn lapio Menez Hom, a'r milwyr
wrthi'n hawlio rhyw lun o arglwyddiaeth
ar ddirgelion diamser Argoed
trwy godi coleri rhag lleithder Medi
pan glywyd rhu'r tanciau'n malu'r grug a'r banadl
ar eu ffordd i fyny.

Ym mhentref Plounevez-Porzay roedd aroglau crasu bara
a hen ddynion yn cychwyn ar eu taith foreol
at y fainc bren wrth droed Calfaria.
Ond uwchben, ar Menez Hom, cododd yr ehedyddion yn
      sydyn
a daeth ofn yn ddrewdod i'r awyr.

MENEZ HOM

(a hill in Brittany)

Lark song seems suitable.
Two larks, so low is this hill,
rise and rise in the clear blue.

Heather and broom thrust
through rusty remnants of that war;
aloof above, in seemly flight,
other birds pass over the quiet hill.

Thirty years since, autumn mists
already low on Menez Hom, military
rites were glumly observed
in Arthur's forest, and soldiers, German ones,
turned up their collars against the cold.

In the village of Plounevez–Porzay
there was baking of bread,
old men mumbled morning offices
on a bench beneath their Calvaire.

Above, larks rose suddenly, approaching tanks,
American ones, could be heard crushing
heather and broom as they came.

Cyn cinio roedd y bechgyn penfelyn
a hudwyd o Frankfurt a Freiburg
i feddiannu bryncyn diolwg
ac i ymbalfalu'n drwsgwl yn yr hen goed
am ferched tywyll Ploueven
yn orffennol blêr ar y concrit
a'u gwaed digenedl eisoes yn baent sych.

Ar Menez Hom, cerddais y gwellt croyw
yn yr haul, heb adael unrhyw farc gwaed
na cherfio allan o amser unrhyw gofeb,
ond roedd caniad ehedydd yn agor llwybr
trwy amser i'r dirgel fyd
lle mae taerineb adar cerdd
a phensaernïaeth dail
yn chwilio hanfod y chwedlau prydferth a chreulon
a grëwyd gan ddynion erstalwm ymysg y coed.

A'r fellten a glywais?
A'r waedd a welais yn yr adfail?
Dychwelais i'r pant lle y bu'r gwaed yn trochi
ac nid oedd undim yno
ond y gwanwyn gwirion yn gwenu
a'r banadl a'r grug yn tyfu.

Long before baking was done, the shivering boys,
chill on their hill, dreaming of warm girls,
aflame in Arthur's wood, lay dead,
their blood on the concrete,
cold as the rain.

I too, a visitor from foreign parts,
trod coarse grass in the sun,
but left no blood.

BEIRDD CANOL OED

(wedi darllen adolygiad gan fardd ifanc ar fy ngwaith i
a gwaith rhai o'm cyfoedion)

Fel ar noson wyntog, y cymylau llwyd
yn llifo dros wyneb y lloer, a Seren
y Gogledd ei hunan yn ansafadwy,
felly y mae beirdd canol oed yn gweld y sêr.
Ysbeidiol, fflachiog ydynt, fel goleudai.
Anaml y mae'r awyr yn glir,
os disglair iawn o hyd y seren annisgwyl
sy'n saethu trwy'r bwlch pan ddaw.

Y mae beirdd canol oed wedi gweld
meidroldeb yn syllu o'r drych
yn y bore, wedi clywed y chwerthin
yn tewi, ac wedi dysgu goddef
yr annigonol. Maent wedi'u llethu
gan y gwacter yn llygaid meirwon tad a mam,
ac wedi teimlo'r oerfel a ddaw pan dorrir
y cortyn a gadael y cwch i lithro i'r dwfn.

Hyn am feirdd canol oed. Y tristwch yw,
a bywyd fel ag y mae,
y gorau y gall bardd ifanc obeithio amdano
yn nhreigl amser
yw bod yn fardd canol oed.

MIDDLE-AGED POETS

(having read a review of my work, and that of my
contemporaries, by a young poet)

As, on a windy night, sparse clouds
stream across the face of the moon
and even the North Star is unstable,
so middle-aged poets see the stars –
momentary, spasmodic as lighthouses.
Nor is the sky often clear,
even if the unheralded beam
of a sudden star still shines brightly.

Middle-aged poets have seen
mortality peering from mirrors
in the morning, have heard laughter
silenced, have learnt to tolerate
the incomplete. They have been wearied
by empty eyes of dead fathers and mothers,
have felt the cold that chills
when ropes are cast and boats
float out into the deep.

This then of middle-aged poets.
Sadly, life being what it is,
the most a young poet can hope for
in the swirl of time
is to be a middle-aged poet.

DU A GWYN – GAEAF 1982

Nos a bore, ar draws y cae gwyn,
aethom ein dau y gaeaf hwnnw.
Roedd y gwynt yn arw a phlu'r eira'n chwerw
a'u llafnau'n fain.
               Âi hithau ar y blaen
bob amser, y bwced fwyd yn drom a thrwsgwl
yn ei dwy law, gan fytran wrth fynd,
mor fach yn y mwrllwch mawr.
Y noson gyntaf, a'r düwch chwyrn yn rhuo o'n cwmpas,
meddyliem, y ddau ohonom, ei fod wedi marw,
wedi rhewi yno'n ddigyfaill.
Ac yna fe'i gwelsom, mor llonydd â cherflun,
yn geffyl gwyn gan eira,
nid mewn unrhyw guddfan ddiogel
ond ar ganol y cae gwyn,
ei lygaid crwn yn goch gan ddewrder ac ofn.
Aeth hi ato a'i dywys, yn nannedd y ddrycin,
gam wrth gam i'r murddun lle bu am wythnosau.
Ninnau, nos a bore, yn troedio tuag ato
ar draws y cae gwyn,
i'w gysuro a'i fwydo.

Daeth tro ar fyd, wrth gwrs, a dyddiau gwyrddion
ond, y gaeaf hwnnw, croesi'r cae gwyn,
dau smotyn du yn erbyn yr awyr lwyd,
oedd bwriad syml ein bod
cyn dod cymhlethdod drachefn
â rhagor o liwiau.

BLACK AND WHITE – WINTER, 1982

Night and morning, across the white field,
the two of us went that winter.
The wind was harsh and the snowflakes bitter,
sharp and biting.
                    She would go on ahead
always, the pail of food heavy and awkward,
held in both hands, and she muttered as she went,
so small in that great gloom.
That first night, white from black roaring around us,
we thought he'd died, frozen friendless.
And then we saw him, monolithic, statuesque,
a horse white with snow,
not sheltering in some corner
but in the open middle of the white field,
his round eyes red with bravery and fear.
She went to him and led him, in the teeth
of the storm, step by step to the ruined shack
where he stayed for weeks.
And we, night and morning, waded towards him
across the white field to feed and comfort him.
The world turned around, of course,
                    and green days came,
but, that winter, the single purpose of
our being was to cross the white
field, two dark specks against the
grey sky, before complexity returned
                    and other colours.

YR EBOL PRES

Y mae gweithred, o'i gwneud, yn dragwyddol,
ac mae'r ebol pres, er mai bustachu i godi y mae,
yn lletywr bellach yn ein tŷ ni'n derfynol.

Tywynnai haul tenau y diwrnod hwnnw,
ond llechai'r llongwr hanner-meddw
ym mhlygion ei gôt wrth gerdded tuag atom.
Fe'i gollyngodd ei hun ar y fainc rhyngom
a nofiodd ei lygaid draw tua'r llongau gwyn
yn y dociau taclus yn Oslo.

Ymhen hir a hwyr, cododd,
a chan droi atat ti'n drwsgwl fonheddig
haliodd yr ebol o ddyfnderoedd ei boced
a'i osod yn dyner yn dy ddwylo.
Yna cerddodd i ffwrdd
i gyfeiriad y dociau taclus
yn ei gôt las.

'Til Nanina, fra Far'
wedi ei grafu'n amrwd ar gefn yr anifail.
Anrheg, mae'n siŵr, meddwn, a luniodd tad i'w ferch
 rhwng twrf y tonnau, yn y nosau hir,
a'i law fawr, gyda gofal manwl,
wedi naddu'r cyhyrau metal i'w atgoffa
am brancio'i gyw merlen o hogan yn yr eira gartre.

Chwarddasom yn ein gyddfau a'i bocedu'n ysgafn,
yr offrwm rhyfedd hwn o ddwylo ffawd.

Heddiw, pe digwyddai'r peth eto trwy oriogrwydd amser,
mi gipiwn i'r ebol oddi arnat
a rhedeg, fy ngwynt yn fy nwrn,
sodro'r ddelw'n ôl yn ei ddwylo cnotiog
a chau'r bysedd am y geiriau a gerfiwyd arno.

THE GIFT

Bronze foal, half-rising,
lodged here in my house for ever.

A thin sun shone
but the drunken sailor,
huddled in a blue trenchcoat,
shivered, shambling towards us.

He sat on the bench, big in the gap between us,
eyes swimming beyond the white ships
in the tidy docks of Oslo.
Soon, unsteady, he rose,
turned, clumsily courteous,
tugged at it, fumbling in a deep pocket,
placed it in your hands.

Then he walked away to the clean docks,
ramrod-blue in his coat.

'Til Nanina, Fra Far'
roughly carved in the smooth belly.
A gift, no doubt, I said, for his daughter,
whittled in the tossing dark
to the hiss of waves on a bulkhead,
his ham hands, with sailor's care,
sculpting lithe limbs, as he called to mind
his foal daughter, light among the snows of home.

We chuckled, young lovers, ready to believe all things,
pocketed our offering from fate.

Had it happened today,
I would have snatched that hostage from your grasp
and ran, breathless, after him

Ond mae gweithred, o'i gwneud, yn dragwyddol.
Mae'r ebol ar godi ar fy nesg i heno,
glaw Gorffennaf yn swp sâl ar y ffenest,
oergri'r mor yn y Borth yn chwithig o'r pellter,
a merch fel cyw merlen ynghwsg yn ei gwely uwchben –
hithau hefyd
ond dros amser yn unig
yn lletya yn y tŷ hwn.

placed it in traitor hands
and closed their fingers over words they had carved.

It lies, half-rising, on my desk tonight,
July rain weeping along my window,
the weary sea hoarse in the distance,
and my daughter, foal-like, asleep above.
She too, but not forever,
lodged in my house.

PRIDD GAEAF

Rwy'n llenwi'r lle â'm chwerthin
am dy fod;
ac am dy fod, fod gobaith.

Lle mae'r coed yn grin
a llun tranc ar foncyff pren
a'r rhew yn is na'r gwreiddiau
ganol gaeaf,
gwelaf un sbrigyn lloerig
ar goll mewn cornel annisgwyl,
a hwnnw'n wyrdd.

Felly tithau,
ac ni allaf beidio â gweiddi
a lluchio cylchau
ac agor drysau
llawenydd
lle cei lifo i mewn heb ofn
a'r lli'n dylifo chwerthin.

WINTER SOIL

I fill the place with laughter
because you are;
and because you are, there's hope.

Where the wood is withered
and the form of death fouls the treestump
and frost creeps beneath the roots
in the dead of winter,
I saw one lunatic twig
lost in an unseen corner,
and it was green.

And so with you.
And I cannot refrain from shouting
and tossing my hat
and opening doors
of happiness
where you can flow in without fear
and the flood drips with laughter.

COED

Y mae coed fel angylion

yr oedd criw o gwmpas fy nghartref
ac ynddynt adar yn nythu'n ddu
a'u siarad yn suro'r nos
                    er na wrandewais

yr oedd coed o gwmpas fy nghartref
a'u brigau'n ddewr heb ddail
a'r awyr yn goch gan ddicter a gwaed angau
                    er nad edrychais

mae coed yn amddiffyn cartref,
yn ymgasglu'n dorf warcheidiol gefn nos
ac yn gwadu hawl y gwynt

ac yn fy ngwely
                    er na sylwais
yr oeddwn innau'n gwybod hynny.

TREES

Trees are like angels

there was a crowd about my home
and in them birds nested black
and their chattering soured the night
        although I did not listen

there were trees about my home
and their branches brave without leaves
and the sky red with anger and death's blood
        although I did not look

trees defend a home
they gather, a protective host, at night,
deny the wind's right

and in my bed
        although I did not notice
I too knew this

TACHWEDD, 1960

Aeth mis cyfan heibio fel lleidr bywyd,
ac yn awr mae Tachwedd yn y coed.

Y tu mewn, lle mae oglau difodiant
a briwiau'n gymysg â chwerthin braf
mewn ystafell glaf, lle mae'r nyrs a'i gwên Leonardo
a'i hwyneb tangnefedd yn gwenu marwolaeth i'w dranc,
y tu mewn, fel plentyn yn gwasgu trwyn ar ffenestr siop,
fe syllwn innau'n wancus trwy'r gwydr oer
ar fyd mor bell o'm cyrraedd.
Fy Moreol Weddi oedd gweld gyda'r brith belydr cyntaf
holl fap y ddinas yn araf ymagor islaw –
a'm Gosber oedd edrych ffarwel ar y lampau'n diffodd
ar ddiwrnod mor hir, a'r byd yn diflannu.

Y tu mewn, yn y nos, pan fo'r chwyrnu trafferthus
yn cydio sawl gwely wrth wely
mewn cymdeithas ryfedd dros dro, mae'r meddwl yn
            crwydro.
Ac yno, ar y blanced antiseptig, dros y gwely digwsg,
mae'r dychymyg yn cynnal gwledd.
                    Hen gyfeillion a hen drafod
a chymdeithas Bangor yn nyddiau coleg,
sgyrsio a chanu a charu yn sgil Sili-wen,
a phopeth gwyrdd a fu'n gyfryw i lwytho bywyd,
gorlwytho bywyd, fel hen drol, hyd at yr ymylon,
a'i anfon i rowlio o brofiad i brofiad, o gornel i gornel,
dan bwysau dyddiau parablus; rhedodd y cyfan,
yn griw afreolus, i yrru'r nos tua'r bore.

Yna, pan ddychwelai'r dydd, cawn innau syllu
drachefn ar y byd na ellid ei gael.
Bychan oedd popeth yno, yn y byd cysglyd
a geisiai ymddangos mor effro am chwech o'r gloch y bore:

NOVEMBER, 1960

A whole month has gone, stolen from time,
now November's in the woods.

Inside, where the smells of decay
and blood mingle with laughter
in the sickroom, where the nurse with the Leonardo smile
and serene face smiles death to death,
inside, like a child pressing his nose to the shop window,
I would stare, hungry through the cold glass,
at a world so far out of reach.
My Mattins to see at the first grey light
a city mapped out below
and my Evensong to take leave of the lights going out
on so long a day and that world fading away.

Inside, in the pit of night, troubled snores
linking bed to bed in that transient community
there, on the antiseptic blanket, over the sleepless bed,
old friends gather and old conversations and college days,
chatter and song and lovemaking in the shades of Siliwen,
and all green things that loaded life, overloaded life,
          like an old farmcart
and sent it rambling from occasion to occasion,
driving the night towards dawn.

Then, when day returned, I would stare once more at
          a world out of reach.
Everything in it was small, in the sleepworn warmth
struggling to awake at six in the morning

a phob dydd y mwg yn ymdroelli uwchben y tai,
yn oedi am eiliad, fel un yn synhwyro'r awyr
am law, neu rybudd, ac yna'n cychwyn, yn ddigon araf,
ar ei daith droellog tua'r môr.

Ac yn nes at y ffenestr, brodwaith darfodedig y coed:
ond hir oedd y coed eleni i golli eu dail;
draw yn y parc, gleision oeddynt o hyd,
diolch i'r nefoedd, o hyd.

Ond yn awr, allan yma, daeth Tachwedd i'r coed
yn ein pentref ni, a minnau'n gawr yn ei ganol.
Heddiw, yn ias y bore, yn y bore byw hwn,
mae popeth yn brydferth a phawb yn gyfaill;

yma'n cropian ger y ffos, 'rwyf innau'n rhan o'r byd;
mae'r danadl bellach mor dyner â'r rhosyn
a chrawc brân yn salm i gomedi bywyd.

Wedi'r mis tywyll, daeth Tachwedd llwydwedd i'r coed,
ac ni bu erioed Dachwedd mor ddifyr â hwn.

and everyday the smoke swirled above the houses,
waited momentarily, as one scents the air
for rain, or for danger, and then setting off, slowly enough,
on its meandering journey to the sea.

Nearer the window, the worn tapestry of the trees;
but the trees this year were late losing their leaves;
over in the park they were green, thank heaven, still green.

And now, November has come to the woods
in our village, and I a giant within it.
Today, in the sharp morning, in this living morning,
all is beautiful, everyone a friend;
creeping along the hedge, I too am a part of the world;
the broom is as delicate as a rose, and the crow's croak
a psalm to life's comedy.

After the black month, grey November has come to the
   woods,
and there was never a November as merry as this.

GORLLEWINO

Nis gwn.
Beth yw teithio i'r dwyrain
a gwybod pendantrwydd
y gwynt digyfaddawd hwnnw?

    Cyrchu'r gorllewin
a wnes wrth gartrefu erioed.

Ac am y rhai
    sy'n mynd am y gogledd
a'u coleri'n wyn gan eira –
nid o'r un hil y maent;
teithiant adref
      yn gryno
      yn alwedigaethol
a gwynt y rhew
    wedi hen ledreiddio eu crwyn.

Cyrchais innau'r gorllewin
    lle mae'r melyn yn gyfrwys
a mesur curiadau amser yn amwys
a chwestiynau'n hofran uwch gorwel y dydd.

    Ond oes i'r gogleddwyr yw hi,
yr ymgyrchwyr pwrpasol
    i eglurder y gogledd.

Cyn hir fe'n cesglir
    mewn faniau twt
a'n gyrru i benrhyn gwyntog
      anhygyrch
        uwchben y môr

WESTERING

I do not know
what it is to travel east
to know the directness
of that uncompromising wind

I have always headed west
when travelling home

(And as for those
  who head northwards
their collars white with snow –
they are not of the same race;
they travel home
                    tidily
                    pursuing their calling
and the icy wind
has long since leathered their skins)

I've gone towards the west
where yellow's deceptive
and the march of seconds ambiguous
and questions hover above the day.

Before long we'll be collected
in tidy vans
and driven to some inaccessible
windy headland overlooking the sea

a'n ffensio,
                a'n gadael –
y rhai sydd â haint gorllewino
                yn pylu
                unplygrwydd eu gweld –
a meini am ein gyddfau rwber.

Dwyreiniwch, ddiawled,
                     neu,
peidied â bod,
                y sawl nad yw'n gweld
ond trwy ddrych
                mewn dameg.

and fenced in
and left –
those whose straightforward vision
is tainted by the plague of the west –
with rocks tied to our rubber necks

Go east, they'll shout, you sods,
  or cease to exist,
you who can only see
through a glass darkly

PISTYLL

Elfen dros elfen. Ymhlyg? Na, o haenen
i haenen hen, caeth yw amynedd craig:
mudandod yw ei hanfod; ynghudd ynddi mae cneuen
y creu cyntaf, yn farw neu'n disgwyl byw,
       fel mewn bru di-had neu fedd gwraig.

Ond am ddŵr, mae'n rhydd. Y rhaeadr a red
dros lwynau'r graig; a'r dafnau sy'n torri
ar ei llyfnder islaw, ail-unir beunydd eu gweddau afrifed;
mae'r dŵr yn chwarae mig â hi, mae'n ei phlagio,
       mae'n chwerthin; mae'n drech na'r cwymp drosti.

Fel gŵr a gwraig, ymnyddu'n ddiflino wnânt
heb obaith uno; tragwyddol anghyflawn
eu hymdrech hwythau, tragwyddol rwystredig eu chwant.
Os maith taerineb dŵr, hirymarhous pob craig
       heb ildio fyth i'r cenna powld ei chyfrinach lawn.

WATERFALL

Element over element. Woven together? No, from stratum
to ancient stratum, the rock's patience is captive;
its essence is silence, hidden within is the kernel
of the first creation, dead or waiting to live,
                    as in a seedless womb or a woman's grave.

But as for water, it is free. The waterfall runs
over the rock's loins; and the drops that splinter
on her smoothness below, their numberless forms are always
re-united;
water plays hide and seek with her, harasses her,
                    and it laughs, it survives its fall over her.

Like man and woman, they weave tirelessly together
with no hope of being one; eternally incomplete
is their effort too, eternally frustrated their desire.
If the persistence of water is vast, long-suffering is every
rock,
        never yielding to the bold rascal its complete secret.

Note: Dŵr (water) is a masculine noun in Welsh, and craig (rock)
is feminine.

EBRILL

Edrychais trwy'r gwydr ddoe ar hap
a gweld un goeden yn wen.
Gaeaf oedd hi o hyd yn y tŷ,
pry' cop yn cysgu, a thân, a chwip
y dwyrain yn brysur, ond trwy'r gwydr
gwelais goeden yn wen
gan flodau afalau.

Bûm ddall ers dyddiau.
Ni wyddwn fod y gwanwyn wedi dod;
ac fel hyn y daw bob amser,
yn debyg i ddyn ansicr o'i groeso,
dyn rhy swil i frolio'i ddod.
Ynghanol fy ngaeaf, yn blasu'r haf
mewn clap o lo neu gerdd,
roeddwn i'n rhy brysur i'w gwrdd.

Ond ddoe ar hap
daeth fy ngaeaf innau i ben;
gwelais un goeden yn wen
gan flodau afalau.

APRIL

Through glass, by chance,
glancing, I saw a white tree.
Winter still inside, a spider asleep,
a fire and the east
wind busy at the window panes,
but through glass I saw a tree
white with apple-blossom.

Been blind for days.
Didn't know that spring had come.
It's how it always comes,
a boy uncertain of his welcome.

Wrapped in winter, sipping summer
in fire's fix or a poem,
I never greeted him.

Yesterday, by chance,
winter ended.
There was this tree,
White with apple blossom.

CARIAD

Mae'r gair yn ddealladwy
mewn termau mân yn unig;
Yma heno, yn nhermau
tân a gwely
ac ystafell nad yw'n dywyll,
yfory hwyrach mewn gwên
ar wyneb na fu'n brydferth o'r blaen.

Ond sut mae cyfundrefnu
a'i osod lle mae'r plant marw
yn gorwedd dan y rhesi gwyn,
er mor gynnes eu haelwydydd hwythau
cyn y dymchwel ofnadwy?
Diau nad oes ystyr i eiriau
lle mae'r gwynt yn oer dros y trothwy.

LOVE

We can understand
only in minor ways.

Here tonight, in terms
of a fire, a bed
and a room that is not dark.
Tomorrow perhaps in a smile
on a face that had not hitherto
been beautiful.

But how to generalise?
To know it where dead children
lie beneath white slabs,
however sweet their cradle-songs
before that terrible destruction?

God knows the word has no meaning
when winds blow cold on hearth-stones.

ONI FU FARW EISOES

Oni fu farw eisoes
fe dyf yn y lleoedd llonydd
ddaioni'r galon syml.

Oni ddaeth tranc drwy'r trafael
ac oni fu farw'r llun
gan ormod lliwiau
fe ddaw tangnefedd ei nwyf
lle nad oes ond bryn.

Oni fu farw'r gair
gan fwrlwm geiriau
gall ei fod yma'n fyw
lle mae'r afon hithau'n
byrlymu swn.

Oni fu farw'r galon ei hunan
ar y ffordd
          cyn cyrraedd.

UNLESS IT IS DEAD

Unless it is dead already,
the simple heart's goodness
may grow in the still places.

Unless death came in that struggle
and unless the picture died
under its weight of colours
peace may come
where there is nothing but a bare hillside.

Unless the Word died
in the torrent of words,
it may be that it lives here,
where, however, the river too
tumbles with sound.

Unless the heart itself died on the way.

REQUIESCAT

(er cof am fy mam)

1

Y mae carreg fedd ym mynwent Tai Duon,
llech uwch eirch plant. Yno'n y gaeaf ag oerwynt
yn hollti dros ysgwydd Graig Goch, mae'r glaw'n golchi
eu henwau, o hyd yn dyfnhau'r hen dristwch gynt.

A phan ddaw haul ifanc Mehefin drwy'r adwy
o'r ffridd i lonni'r dail a'r gwair o'i chwmpas hi,
bron na chlywir eu chwerthin ymysg y meini
a'u traed yn ysgeifn ar gwsg eu cyfoedion hwy.

Es â hi yno yn yr haf, ac edrychodd
ar yr enwau, brodyr a chwiorydd ei mam
a fu farw o dlodi yn blant. Hwn oedd y cam
a wnaed â'r werin – angau plant. Ochneidiodd. Trodd.
"Y petha bach. Fel 'na roedd hi." Daeth ei llais o bell.
"Wyt ti'n meddwl, wir, yr aethon nhw i wlad sy well?"

2

Yr oedd llun ei thad bob amser wrth law ganddi,
ei safiad hy yn ei siwt rhy fawr a'i fwstas
yn herio'r teclyn newydd. Ym mhentre Pant Glas,
yn fychan a gwydn, trwsio a phedoli
yn ogof gymdogol ei efail oedd cylchfin
ei ddyddiau. Cludai hithau ei fwyd a'i de ddeg
a gwylio'r hogiau'n cadw riad. Pe câi osteg,
âi ef ar ei feic mawr i gyrrau Bwlchderwin
a'r Bwlch Mawr i ysgwyd llaw a chasglu'r biliau
na hawliodd yn ystod y misoedd llwm.

REQUIESCAT

(in memory of my mother)

1

There is a gravestone in the cemetery at Tai Duon,
slate above child coffins. There in the winter with chill wind
splitting its way over Graig Goch's shoulder, the rain washes
their names, further deepening the old old sadness.

And when the young sun of June comes through the gap
from the moor to liven the leaves and grass,
their laughter might be heard between the stones
and their feet, light upon companion's sleep.

We went there, she and I, in the Summer, and she gazed
at their names, brothers, sisters,
who died in poverty as children. This was the wrong
visited upon the commoner – the death of children.
    She sighed. Turned.
"Poor things. That's how it was," – her voice from far away –
"Do you really think that they went to a better place?"

2

Her father's photograph always at hand, his bold
stance in his oversize suit, moustache challenging
the new-fangled gadget. In the village of Pant Glas,
small and sturdy, shoeing and mending in the sociable
cave of his smithy filled his days. She would bring
bread and tea there and eye the lads. On a slack day
he would mount his huge bicycle to Bwlchderwin and Bwlch
Mawr to pump hands and claim payment not claimed in

Nid oedd yn cadw cyfrif. Ond eisoes roedd drwm
yr ymgyrch ricriwtio'n curo yng nghlustiau'r hogiau –
fe'u denai o hir undonedd y gwair a'r ŷd
i fartsio fel moch Gadara dros ddibyn byd.

3

Miri mawr! Crymffastiau'r ganrif newydd mewn car
modur yn rhuo o bentref i bentref am ugain
milltir yr awr. Yn rhochian, yn sgrytian, yn ubain
dros ffyrdd y wlad, hwy oedd uchelwyr y lonydd di-dar.
Rhyddid rhyfedd cyflymder yn herio amser –
mor aml yn y ffos ag ar y ffordd, gwthio
mor aml â gyrru, chwilota a sgriwio
dan foneti, plant balch y peiriant diager.

Hithau'n bert ar biliwn moto-beic ei brodyr,
a'r gwynt yn gweu trwy ei gwallt. Bryd hyn roedd tlodi
a'i bryder wedi'i drechu, antur yn gyffur;
nid oedd dros dro ynghlwm wrth gaethiwed cyni.
Dros y corsydd llaith, mor hen â'r Mabinogi,
y rhain oedd ei meirch dihangol a'i harwyr hi.

4

Coflaid a chusan wrth loetran o Ffair Llanllyfni,
adref yn giang yng ngolau'r lloer; roedd hyn hefyd
yn rhan o'r patrwm – cymowta o stryd i stryd
yn Y Dre, gennod y wlad yn bwrw iddi.

Yna daeth Jôs – llygaid duon, gwallt slic, sgidiau sglein –
o rywle pell fel Llanbêr i stesion Pant Glas.
Un o hogiau'r chwarel oedd Jôs, mwy sbriws na gwas
ffarm, yn stydio'n y nos yn ei focs wrth y lein,

the lean months. He never kept accounts. But already
the recruiting drum was beating in young men's ears,
enticing them from the long monotony of hay
and corn to march, Gaderene swine, over the world's precipice.

3

Great excitement! The likely lads of the new century
roaring from village to village in a motor car at
twenty miles an hour. Grunting, shaking, hooting
over the country roads. The aristocrats of
the untamed lanes. Speed is freedom
challenging time – in the ditch as often as on the
road, pushing as often as driving, hunting and
scrabbling under bonnets, the proud children of the
steamless engine. And she, pretty on her brothers'
pillions, wind weaving through her hair.
Poverty was defeated then, adventure a drug; for
a while, not enslaved by need. Over the damp
marshland, old as the Mabinogi, these were her
trusty steeds, her heroes.

4

Embraces and kisses, loitering home from Llanllyfni
Fair, a merry gang in the moonlight; this too was
part of the pattern – strolling from street to street
in The Town, the country girls setting to. Then came
Jones – black eyes, slicked-down hair, shiny shoes –
from some faroff place like Llanberis to Pant Glas
station. Jones was one of the quarry lads, more spruce
than the farm boys, studying at night in his signalbox
by the line, home full of himself, a sergeant,

wedi dod adra'n jiarff, yn sarjant, o'r rhyfel,
a'i fryd ar fynd yn Berson. Rhai felly oeddynt,
ffroenuchel, anfodlon eu byd, hogiau'r chwarel
– digon o glep, fel stalwyn am ferch, dim heb bunt
neu ddwy yn y boced fel arfer. Priododd hithau Jôs;
a thynnu llun yng Ngh'narfon yn bropor ei phôs.

5

Dau geffyl mewn cae, rwy'n cofio, ôl mwyara
ar fy ngwefl a'm crys, a'r dyrnaid a gorlannwyd
i'r piser bach yn ddigon oer i ddal annwyd,
chwedl f'ewyrth. Fel y gwrychoedd a'r coed 'fala,
gwyrai'r ddau i'r un awel a chwaraeai drostynt.
Mor llonydd hir y safent, llonyddais innau
ac yn chwistlo'n isel a gwylio'u clustiau,
eu clustiau'n unig, yn codi'n ofnus i'r gwynt.

Hithau'n llenwi'r piser mawr, o'r gwrych, yn y gwair,
ffon fagl yn bachu'r cangau uwch, naws hydref
o'r diwedd yn gyrru'r ddau biser tuag adref.
Ac fel y cerddem, law-yn-llaw heb yngan gair,
safai'r ceffylau'n ddu yn erbyn y machlud;
maent yno'n warcheidwaid pur, disymud o hyd.

6

Mrs-Jôs-y-Person fyddai hi bellach,
a Jôs fyddai yntau i'w theulu am byth.
Gorchwyl gwraig oedd ei gwaith, gosod lliain yn syth
ar allor, chwythu'r harmoniwm, dioddef llach
gŵr a addolai am adael i'w chreadur
o fab dyfu'n rhydd, yn llo Llŷn, a'i swcro
i dreulio'i amser dragywydd yn seiclo
o fyd y Person at hud ei brodyr.

from the war, bent on becoming a Parson. That's what
they were like, arrogant, dissatisfied with their lot, the
quarry lads – plenty of lip, stallions for the girls,
not without a pound or two in their pockets.
So she married Jones, and was photographed
in Caernarfon in a suitable pose.

5

Two horses in a field I remember, blackberry stains
on my mouth and my shirt, and the handful safely
penned in the small can lonely enough to catch cold, as my
uncle would say. Like the hedgerows and the apple-trees, both
leaned into the same breeze that played over them. So
still they stood for so long, I became still also and then
whistled quietly and watched their ears, only their ears,
pointing up into the wind. She filled the large can,
from the hedgerow, in the long grass, a crooked stick
hooking the higher clumps, and the sharpness of
autumn finally driving the two cans home. And as
we walked, hand in hand without a word,
the horses stood black against the sunset; they
are there still, pure, motionless watchmen.

6

She'd be Mrs Jones-Parson from now on, and
Jôs is what he'd be to her family for ever. Her
work was women's work, straightening the
altarcloth, pumping the harmonium, enduring her adored
husband's lash for allowing her son to grow wild –
a Llŷn calf – encouraging him to spend his time
cycling from the Parson's world to the magic of her brothers'.

Fe'i cipiwyd ef o'r diwedd o'i gofal hi
i'w feithrin yn 'gent' yn Lloegr, a'i gadael
oriau hir mewn ficerdai gwag, sgrech brân, cri
tylluan ei hunig gwmni'n aml. Cael
trip i Lerpwl oedd ei thâl, pâr o sgidiau
smart a het, eu dangos ar y Sul a'u mwynhau.

7

Daeth i arfer. A doedd bywyd ddim yn ddrwg,
wedi'r cyfan, rhwng dau − Jôs oedd o o hyd.
Er cased cofio'r mab yn ei ysgol ddrud,
roedd hynny er lles, siŵr o fod, ac roedd mwg
yn codi o'r simnai i'w gyfarch adref.
Ymgartrefodd yn Llŷn, a chadwai gyswllt
â'i mam a'i brodyr, a phrynu gwerth deuswllt
o betrol i ffytian ei ffordd tua'r 'Nef'.

Aeth rhyfel arall heibio, ond nid yn Llŷn.
Daeth hithau'n gelfydd i addurno allor
â gwaith ei llaw. Bellach fe dyfodd yn un
â'i swyddogaeth. Aeth o Lŷn i Fôn, a'i hangor
oedd bod yn driw i'w safle a byw'n ddi- stŵr,
gwneud te i'r Deon Gwlad a charu ei gŵr.

8

Yna daeth gwacter. I bawb mae'r gyflafan
bersonol yn fwy na rhuadau canrif.
I hi roedd yn nos faith. Ceisiodd rhoi cyfrif,
drosodd a throsodd, o'i dranc. Yn ei berllan,
dan ei goed, fe'i lladdwyd. Disgynnodd wifren
fyw mewn storm a chynnau tân mewn twmpath dail;

He was snatched away eventually to become a
gent in England, leaving her long hours in empty
vicarages, the croak of crows, the hoot of an owl
often her only company. A trip to Liverpool an
occasional reward, smart shoes and a hat,
showing them off on Sundays and enjoying them.

7

She got used to it. And life wasn't bad, after
all, for the two of them – he was still Jones.
Hard though it was to think of her son in that
expensive school, it was for the best, no doubt,
and smoke still rose from the chimney to welcome him
home. She made her home in Llŷn, kept contact
with her mother and brothers, and bought two shillings
worth of fuel to putter her way to 'Heaven'.
Another war passed but not in Llŷn. And she
became expert at decorating altars with her own
handiwork. She had become one with her function. She
went from Llŷn to Anglesey, and her anchors
were to be true to her status and live an
unruffled life, make tea for the Rural Dean
and love her husband.

8

Then an empty void. To everyone the personal
catastrophe is more than the century's disasters.
For her it was a long night. She tried to explain
his death, over and over. In his orchard, beneath his
trees, he was killed. A live cable came down in
a storm and started a fire in a pile of leaves; Jones

hen igam-ogamu rhwng cân a chariadon,
cyplau llwyd yn chwysu mewn siwtiau, swyn y don
yn denu pawb. Wfftia hi'r Pwnsh a Jiwdi –
"Lol wirion! Dydi rhai petha'n newid dim!"
Ac ymlaen i brynu fferins a hufen iâ –
gwyn, wrth gwrs, nid rhyw hen binc – "Gwyn ydi eis
      crîm."
Ac adre'n ôl at y lleill yn eu cadeiria.

Hen wraig eto'n ferch fach, allan am dro, a had
ei bru'n ei hebrwng – y mab erbyn hyn ydi'r tad.

EPILOG

Gwytnwch eiddilwch oedd, pob modfedd ohoni.
Fe'i crëwyd o gyni, corsen fain yn tyfu
mewn tir llaith, heb fod ganddo'r maeth i'w haeddfedu.
Ond o storm i storm a thrwy'r hirlwm dal ati
oedd ystyr bod a phwrpas bodolaeth iddi.

Ac o fynd, i ninnau'n weddill tyfodd yn fwy,
fel y gwna'r meirw. Fel cyw petrus yn codi
o'r nyth, mewn syndod mud ehedant yn ddi-glwy
i'r ehangder mawr o gyrraedd ein galar ni.

Tua'r diwedd, daeth colomennod at ei ffenest
fel pe baent yn dwyn tystiolaeth ar derfyn dydd
i rym eu heiddilwch hwy, neu'n cludo amnest
am bopeth croes. Bu'n gaeth. Goroesodd. Aeth yn rhydd.

weaving the chair among lovers and the bandstand
music, grey couples sweaty in suits, the sea
beguiling all. She snorted at the Punch and Judy:
'Silly nonsense; some things don't change at all!'
And on to buy sweets and ice-cream –
white, of course, not some fancy pink – 'Ice-cream
is white.' Then back home to the others in
their easy chairs. An old lady became a little girl
once more, out for a walk, and the seed of her
womb – the son by now is the father.

EPILOG

Tough she was in her frailty, every inch of her.
She was created in poverty, a thin reed growing
in damp earth that hadn't the richness to nourish her.
But from storm to storm and through the long drought
holding on was the meaning of being and the
purpose of existence for her.

And when she went, to us who remained, she grew
greater, as the dead do. Like nervous fledglings rising
from their nest, in mute wonderment they fly unharmed
into the great expanse out of reach of our grief.

Towards the end, doves came to her window
as though bearing witness at the day's end
to the power of their frailty,
of bringing amnesty for all that was
wrong. She was captive. She endured. She was set free.

PYMTHEG

Heddiw mae'n bymtheg
a'r tu ôl i'r llygaid gofalus
sy'n cynnig ac eto'n cadw,
yng nglendid y tân sy'n tasgu
o'r cyhyrau glas –
prydferthwch ebol ar garlam
trwy wlith y bore –
mae'n nes at ddelwedd Duw
na fu ac na fydd
yn y wisg farwol hon.

Mae'n falchder bedwen

Mae'n bysgotwr yn nŵr afon
lle mae pysgod mawr
na ellir fyth eu dal.
Heddiw mae'n bymtheg.

BIRTHDAY

Behind the careful eyes that offer
and yet hold back,
in the purity of the flame
that burns through green sinews
– the purity of a colt galloping
in the morning – he is nearer
God's image than he has been
or will be in this mortal dress.
He is the suppleness of a birch-tree.
He is a fisherman in a river
where there are great fish
that will never be caught.

He is fifteen.

DARLUN O'R CYFNOS

LLEFARYDD 1:
Mae'r tyfiant yn cerdded y tir yn glywadwy,
yn meddiannu ffordd-lâs a ffordd-drol dros nos,
y gwair a'r planhigion-cywilydd-fy-merch,
yr ŷd cyn uched â choeden,
y coediach, y bwrlwm yn drech ym mhobman.

LLEFARYDD 2:
Yn y gwely, ym mol y nos, gwrandewch,
Mae'n cerdded y tir,
yn marchogaeth gwartheg a llyffantod
o borfa-hyd-coes i borfa sy'n goedwig cricedau,
ac yn sleifio at ochr y gwely
fel y sleifia dŵr mewn hunllef
yn benderfynol oer a llyfn...

Sŵn cwpanau'n tincial, mân chwerthin a lleisiau merched.

Siwgwr yn eich coffi, Mrs Ym?
Mi fyddan nhw'n gofyn pedair punt nesa.
Welsoch chi f'un i'n treio ista'n y seti gora Dydd Sul?
Fel na maen 'nhw.
Ac isio sgidia i'r plant medda hi. Fel tasa ganddi hi ddim.
Na, dydyn nhw ddim run fath.
Beth dach chi'n i ddisgwyl? Siwgwr yn ych coffi,
        Mrs. Ym? Siwgwr yn ych coffi, Mrs Ym?
Mae nhw'n dweud fod morynion o'r wlad yn haws.
Fasa hi ddim wedi cael gwneud petha fel'na ers talwm.
Siwgwr yn ych coffi, Mrs Ym?

SELECTIONS FROM 'EVENING, A PORTRAIT'

(an ode for radio)

1ST VOICE:
The power of growth walks the earth audibly,
possesses paths and tracks overnight,
coarse grass and shame-on-my-daughter,
corn as tall as trees,
brushwood, everywhere the upthrust conquers.

2ND VOICE:
In bed, in the belly of night, listen,
it stalks the earth,
rides the cattle, the tree-frogs
from knee-high pasture to pasture that's the cricket's forest,
then creeps to your bedside
like water in a nightmare
deliberate, cold and smooth...

The sounds of cups tinkling, laughter and women's voices

Sugar in your coffee, Mrs Ymm?
They'll be asking four pounds next.
Did you see mine trying to sit in the front pews last Sunday?
That's how they are.
And wanting shoes for the children, she said.
As though they had none.
No, they're not the same.
What can you expect?
Sugar in your coffee, Mrs Ymm?
They say maids from the country are easier.
She couldn't have done it in the old days.
Sugar in your coffee, Mrs Ymm?

LLEFARYDD 1:
Awr machlud a'r awyr gwallgof
yn rhuo a'i dwylo ar led,
ei wyneb yn waed, yn gochni dicter nef mewn gwefl,
yn llydan fel difa tas wair yn erbyn y nos,
sgrechian diobaith llyffantod y gwellt,
sŵn yn llachar, lliwiau'n crochlefain,
fel bod tywyllwch, pan ddaw,
yn llawn ac yn bell ac yn canu clychau
ym mhen-draw-byd y nerfau.

LLEFARYDD 2:
Daw'r düwch sydyn
fel ergyd corfforol bob nos;
er y daw bob nos yn ddi-feth,
mae'n ergyd bob tro.
A thrwyddo fel pryfed ar felfed,
yn llinell aflêr ddiderfyn dros riw a goriwaered,
yn gyfres o fân unigolion ar daen dros y ddaear,
mae'r pentrefi'n llusgo adref
o'r farchnad, o'r bar, o gornel stryd,
o iard y dyn gwyn, o'r carchar, o gefnau'r byd,
pawb yn blasu'r nos mewn perlewyg preifat,
pawb yn gweld teithio'n well na chyrraedd,
pob un yn ei gawell ei hun . . .

Nifer o leisiau'n ymdoddi i'w gilydd.

LLEFARYDD 1:
Jim-Jim, ar fy ffordd, mae'n debyg, i rywle;
dim iws, meddan nhw, i neb
ond i ferch a'i dyn oddi cartref;
a myn diawl, be 'di'r ots
os ca'i bres i brynu transistor
ac eistedd yng nghysgod haul
a gwrando ar Sobers yn Lloegr yn maeddu'r Sais?

1ST VOICE:
Sunset hour and the lunatic sky
roars and stretches out his arms,
his face is blood, red as the anger of heaven,
wide as a burning haystack against the night;
the hopeless shriek of frogs in the grass,
sound is lurid, colours bellow out;
darkness, then it comes,
is full and far and rings bells
in the far reaches of the nerves.

2ND VOICE:
The sudden dark
falls like a physical blow each night;
although it comes each night without fail
it's a blow every time.
And through it like flies on velvet,
an endless sprawling line over hill and dale,
a series of lone figures spread over the earth,
the villages drag themselves home
from market, from bars, from street corners,
from the white man's yard, from prison, from the ends of
    the earth.

Voices merge into each other . . .

1ST VOICE:
Jim-Jim, on my way, I suppose, somewhere,
No use, they say, to anyone
but a girl whose man's away;
and what the hell, what matters,
if I can buy a transistor
and sit in the shade
and listen to Sobers in England beating the English?

LLEFARYDD 2:
Hapusrwydd Powel, fy mhen ôl yn sboncio
a'm coesau'n llifo fel mêl;
rwy'n ddu fel jon-crô ac yn gwybod yn iawn
fod Jim-Jim yn llygaid i gyd
a'i ddannedd yn wyn
a'i draed yn hawdd eu nabod ar y lôn . . .

LLEFARYDD 1:
Miriam – fel yn y Beibl – Wilias,
ac yn cofio'n iawn beth yw goglais gwaed
a cherdded fel iâr dandan adref o'r farchnad,
gwybod fod llygaid yn garcus
ac aros yn y gwellt hir yng nghysgod coed bara.
Ond bois bach, rwy'n hen,
ac mae gennyf dan drugaredd Iôr,
mewn carchar yn Spanish Town, ar long yn rhywle,
ar strydoedd Harlem, dan dywarchen werdd yn yr ardd gefn,
dri-ar-ddeg o blant dynion,
digon, wir Dduw, i neb,
ond heno, wrth siglo i'r canu,
bydd y groth yn gryndod o atgof
yn y cwrdd haleliwia . . .

Llais merch yn canu'n ddistaw

Hanner can milltir i Spanish Town,
A'r drws haearn trwm wedi'i gloi,
A'r drws haearn trwm wedi'i gloi.

Hanner can milltir i Spanish Town,
Tair blynedd a'r muriau mor fawr,
O tair blynedd a'r muriau mor fawr.

2ND VOICE:
Happiness Powell, my bottom bouncing
and my legs flowing like honey;
I'm black as John-Crow and know very well
that Jim-Jim's all eyes
and his teeth that white
and I know easy his footsteps on the road . . .

1ST VOICE:
Miriam-like in the Bible-Williams,
but remembering well the itch in the blood
and walking home like a bantam hen
knowing that eyes were watching and waiting
in the long grass under the breadfruit tree.
But, man, I'm so old,
and I have me, in God's mercy,
in a prison in Spanish Town, on a ship somewhere,
on the streets of Harlem, beneath the green sod in my garden,
thirteen children of men,
enough, God knows, for anyone,
but tonight, as I sway to the singing,
my womb will quiver with longing
in the Halleluia meeting . . .

The sound of a girl singing quietly

Half a hundred miles to Spanish Town
And the heavy iron door is locked
Oh, the heavy iron door is locked.

Half a hundred miles to Spanish Town
Three years and the walls are so high
Oh, three years and the walls are so high.

LLEFARYDD 2:
Ar fonyn hen goeden banana
dan gysgod fflam-y-fforest,
merch yn eistedd, Rhosyn Saron,
ac yn troi o'i gylch, fel cŵn yn disgwyl canmoliaeth,
tri picni bach,
dwy leuad eu llygaid yn grynion,
eu boliau tynn, hwythau'r un mor grwn,
yn bochio o'u blaenau fel merched yn disgwyl,
a'u dannedd yn barbareiddio melynder y mango.
Ond pell ei llygaid hi, difater-bell
fel un a welodd angau'n cerdded mewn cnawd
ac a rannodd ei anobaith.

LLEFARYDD 1:
Mae cysgod dyn yn llonydd dan y coed,
ei bwysau'n osgeiddig ungoes;
nid yw'n siarad nac yn symud
ond mae osgo ei gorff yn hysbysebu ei ryw.
Daw'r nos fawr dros y ddau,
a'i chysur a chyfle i anghofio . . .

Miss Yma'n-rhy-hir Brown,
cenhedlaeth o ymatal wedi rhwymo fy nhafod,
mwstas bach dan fy nhrwyn
a sanau gwlân fis Ionawr yn y mynyddoedd.
Gadewais Loegr yn rhy bell o'm hôl
i'r deyrnas lwyd ddi-gyfeiriad ddi-uchelwyr honno
dynnu bellach yn llinynnau fy ngwybod,
er mor eiddgar y darllenaf y *Times* bob dydd
saith niwrnod yn hwyr.
Ac eto beth a wnaf yn yr hinsawdd llachar hwn
ond cerdded yn glòs fy wyneb
heb edrych i'r dde nac i'r aswy
rhwng y perthi hibiscus

2ND VOICE:
On the stump of an old banana tree
in the flame-of-the-forest's shadow,
a girl sits, Rose of Sharon,
and twisting about her, like dogs seeking affection,
three little ones,
the moons of their eyes full,
their bellies tight, just as round as moons,
thrusting ahead like those of pregnant women,
their teeth savaging the golden mango.
But her eyes are far, uncaring far,
like one who has seen death in the flesh
and has shared its hopelessness.

1ST VOICE:
A man's shadow stands beneath the trees,
his weight elegantly on one leg;
he neither speaks nor moves
but his body proclaims his sexuality.
The great night descends on them both
and its comfort and its leave to forget...

Miss Here-too-long Brown,
my tongue tied from years of restraint,
a little moustache beneath my nose
and woollen socks in winter here in the hills.
I have left England too far behind me
for that grey land with no direction
and no aristocracy
to pluck at the strings of my knowing
however eagerly I read the *Times* each morning
seven days late.
And yet what shall I do in this crude climate
but walk carefully to myself
looking neither right nor left
between the hibiscus hedges

i dai fy nhri chyfaill
i gloncian a chwarae cardiau yn fy het . . .

LLEFARYDD 1:
Y drymiau llaw yn dechrau'n araf-dawel,
clic-clac, clic-clac dan ddwylo un neu ddau,
ac ar draws y gwellt, trwy'r gwyll,
cysgodion dyfnion duon gosgeiddig
yn llifo i gyfeiriad yr alwad.

LLEFARYDD 2:
Yna'r sŵn yn cryfhau,
drymiau eraill yn deffro,
y dorf yn crynhoi
y sŵn yn cryfhau,
y cylch yn llenwi,
y dawnsio'n ymysgwyd,
yr hudo'n ymestyn,
y casglu cynnil ar amryw ysbrydion,
y gwallgofi pwrpasol cynlluniedig,
y melltithio patrymog a'r galw ar gythraul.

LLEFARYDD 1:
Ac yno ym mwynder sêr
dan adenydd cynnes y calabash,
eu breichiau'n hollti'r nos
mewn defod benodol fel cerflun,
eu cyrff yn seirff dolennog
heb nac ysbryd na meddwl yn frodyr iddynt,
caethweision y dyfnder a'r gwres
a'r canrifoedd culion dinewid yn yr ynys hon,
yno morynion McAlister a Smith,
Jones a Chung a Brown a Raman Singh,
yngholl i'r realiti llwm o sgwrio Vim mewn tai
a dysgu arferion gwâr y merched gwelw,

to the houses of my three friends
to gossip and play cards in my hat?

1ST VOICE:
The hand drums begin slowly, quietly,
clic-clac, clic-clac, one here, one there,
and across the grass, through the dark,
deep sinuous shadows
pour towards their summons.

2ND VOICE:
Sound strengthens
other drums awake
crowd gathers
sound strengthens
the circle fills
dancing begins
witchcraft reaches out,
the subtle calling up of spirits
the controlled, deliberate madness
the patterned cursing and the summoning of devils

1ST VOICE:
And there under the soft stars
beneath the warm wings of the calabash,
their arms cleaving the night
in a ritual as specific as sculpture
their bodies weaving serpents
with no spirit or mind,
slaves to the deep sound and the heat
and the long narrow centuries in this island
there the maids of McAlister and Smith,
Jones and Chung and Brown and Raman Singh,
are lost to the grey reality of scrubbing,
of enduring the ways of the pale women,

yngholl ac yn gwisgo ar lygaid a gwefus
stamp dychrynllyd y cynfyd.

LLEFARYDD 1:
Ynghanol y dref, cloc yr eglwys yn taro
ei ddeg trawiad araf diddadl,
yn dwyn pwyll i'r tawelwch o'i gwmpas
ac yn gwbl Anglicanaidd
yn nhrymder esgobol ei lais.
Mae'r eglwys yn ddieithryn pwysig
a fu'n westai, gwaetha'r modd, yn rhy hir
heb dalu ei ffordd.

LLEFARYDD 2:
Mae'r siopau'n farw a'r eglwys farw-fawr
yn teyrnasu drostynt,
a'r dyn wedi cilio o'i fachlud-feranda
i Ewrop ei ddodrefn a'i set radio,
ond yn y farchnad mae'r merched a'r plant,
gwragedd solet o Santa Cruz,
merched hirgoes o Christiana
a'r plant nad oes unman arall i'w cadw
yn troi a throsi fel cŵn ar gyfer y nos,
noson y gwrachod a'r jiwc-bocs,
pen ar lwyth o iam,
traed ar y glorian-gartref,
a'r corff yn gyfforddus
rhwng y sachau oren a'r sachau cnau.
Daeth y rhain dros lwybr llwch
o ben-draw'r-plwyf i werthu pan ddaw'r wawr
gynnyrch eu chwys yng nghrastir y gwastadeddau,
eu paciau'n simsan ar eu pennau
a'u llygaid mawr yn llonydd ac annirnad.

lost and bearing in eyes and lips
the terrible stamp of another world . . .

1ST VOICE:
In the centre of the town, the church clock strikes
its ten slow incontestable strokes,
bringing caution to the night around it
the utterly Anglican
in the episcopal heaviness of its voice.
The church is an alien of some importance
who has been a house-guest, sadly, too long
and without paying its way.

2ND VOICE:
The shops are dead and the great dead church
presides over them;
the white man has retreated from his sunset veranda
to the Europe of his furniture and his radio;
but in the market the women and children,
solid wives from Santa Cruz,
long-legged women from Christiana
and children they have nowhere to put them
twist and turn like dogs preparing their beds
for the night, for the night of witchcraft and juke-box music
heads resting on piles of yam,
feet on home-made scales
bodies sort of comfortable
between sacks of oranges and sacks of nuts.
These have walked the dusty paths
from far ends of the parish to sell, come dawn,
the product of their sweat in the arid lowland
their heavy packs on their heads
and their great eyes still and unfathomable.

107

LLEFARYDD 2:
Mae'n nos, ond nid yw'n dawel.
Y tryciau fel troliau'n rholio'u ffordd
trwy'r düwch mawr i fore'r ddinas;
y jiwc-bocs yn nadu i'r tywyllwch
aberthau ei chwecheiniogau,
ambell bwl o chwerthin cras caregog,
a chorws diddosbarth y cŵn yn chwyddo
o blasty i gwt i blasty;
sŵn gwallgof diddiwedd trigolion y glaswellt
a grwndi croesacen rhyw gweryl pell ar y gwynt.

LLEFARYDD 2:
Daeth saib yn y symud,
ond ni ellir goddef distawrydd
lle mae bywyd mor llawn ysbrydion,
a'r hen hen ofnau'n cyniwair mor llachar
trwy wythiennau cymysgryw dynion.

Mae'n nos, ond nid yw'n dawel,
a draw yn y pellter cyfrin
mae'r cwrdd haleliwia'n wylo-ganu
gan gredu fod yn rhywle drugaredd
a deifl yn ei amser ei hun
oleuni'r gwir ar y pethau hyn.

*Sŵn llais yn y pellter yn canu "Cario Ffrwyth Aci" ac yn
graddol ddistewi.*

2ND VOICE:
It's night, but it isn't silent.
The trucks roll their way through the dark
to the city's morning,
juke-boxes wail into the blackness
their sacrificial offerings,
an occasional harsh stony burst of laughter,
the endless classless antiphonies of dogs
swelling from palace to shack to palace;
the crazy perpetual cries of crickets in the grass
and the distant echo of some far quarrel on the wind.

1ST VOICE:
There's a pause in the movement
but silence cannot be endured
where life is haunted by so many spirits
and the ancient fears beat so fiercely
through men's blood.

It's night, but it isn't silent
and in the mysterious distance
the halleluia-meeting's long wailing
expresses its belief that somewhere a mercy
will throw, in its own good time,
the light of truth on all these things.

*A voice in the distance sings "Carry me Ackee", and
gradually fades away.*

GWYDDAU YNG NGREGYNOG

Mae'r gwyddau wedi mynd. Does dim prinder
cynnwrf dros wyneb y llyn: y gotiar
groch ymhongar ar drywydd busneslyd,
ei ffws du'n annifyrru'r llwydni clyd;

yr hwyaid gwylltion mewn dychryn yn codi
a chylchu, cwaa, cwaa, chwipio'r brwyn, cadw
stŵr yn nryswig yr ynys; hen foda
ar adain lonydd, ias oer yn hwyr ha.

Nac oes. Ond y llynges gefnsyth a wyliais
feunos eleni eto'n rhwyfo'n un rhes
drefnus forwrol trwy'r brwyn awr machlud,
magodd adenydd, aeth. Diriaid yw'r byd!

Heb eu hurddas penuchel, amddifad
gwareiddiad llyn. A'r ddelwedd osodwyd
ar wyddau? Mor ffals! Llariaidd rai oeddynt,
mwyn a phrydferth dros ddrych dŵr oedd eu hynt.

Fin nos cerddent yn fintai ofalus
o'u pori yn y gwair tal i'w gwir wanas
yn y pabwyr a'r gellhesg, gan lithro
i'w helfen mor llyfn a meddiannu bro.

Chwe fechain yn frown a bregus, tad balch ar y blaen
yn arwain ac un o'r tu ôl yn fain
ei chonsárn bob eiliad dros y cywion –
teulu organig twt, meithringell gron.

Dros fisoedd y styrbans mewn llyn – clochdar brain,
malais sgrech y coed, trymder deutroed dyn,
hwy oedd yr elfen wâr, dycnwch gwastad
eu meithrin a'u twf yn hawlio parhad.

GEESE AT GREGYNOG

The geese have gone. No lack
of bustle on the lake's surface; coarse
and boastful coot about his black
affairs, busy fuss on the quiet grey;

wild duck ascending in fear,
circling, cwaa, cwaa, whipping the rushes,
creating commotion in the island jungle;
one ominous buzzard watching the summer night.

No lack. But the fleet I have watched
nightly this year once more, sailing in rank,
an orderly progress through reeds at sunset,
it took wing and went. The world's bereft.

Without their dignity, the lake
is stripped of gentility; the stereotype
of geese – how false! Their flow was fluent
on the lake's mirror, it was calm and easeful.

They would proceed at evening, a careful
company, from tall grass grazing
to their true home in the bulrush forest,
and become one with their dwelling –

Six bundles, brown and vulnerable, proud father
leading, and one, long-necked, at the rear,
sharp-nosed in her concern for her chicks,
an organic family, a cellular nursery.

Over months of business on a lake – crows harsh,
jays malicious, man's heavy tread,
they were its civil order, their perseverance,
their daily upbringing willing perpetuity.

Ond heno, ddiwedd haf, mae'r gaea'n agos,
a'i oerni annhymig dirybudd yn ernes
y gwelaf, hwyrach y tro nesaf, ryw wanwyn
pryd na ddaw'r gwyddau fyth eto'n ôl i'r llyn.

But tonight, at summer's end, winter seems near,
its sudden, untimely chill a certain portent
that I shall know, perhaps next year, a spring
when the geese will return no more to the lake.

CAROL

Hon ydyw'r nos y daeth fel brawd,
yn dlawd ac oer, fab Duw heb fri;
Ryfeddaf nos y teithiodd Crist
yn drist o'r nef i'n daear ni.
       Hon ydyw'r nos.

O wyrthiol nos, aeth clebr byd
yn astud fud, fod gwendid pur
trwy lendid triw'n dirfodi trais,
trwy ras yn herio'r galon ddur.
       O wyrthiol nos.

Ofnadwy nos, daeth heulwen bod,
hanfod y byd, at ddynion coll,
a gwaedd a grwndi baban gwan
yn destun cân y nefoedd oll,
       ofnadwy nos.

CAROL

This is the night our brother came,
So poor and cold, God's son unhailed.
The wondrous night he journeyed down
From heavn's high home to our sad world.
      O awful night.

Marvellous night, tumult of earth
Became so still, as purity
In weakness dressed, conquered brute force,
By grace it shamed the hardest heart.
      Marvellous night.

O awful night, the sun of being
Came to this world, to lost mankind,
And one small baby's cradle cry
Makes all the hosts on high to sing.
      O awful night.

Nodiadau / Notes

T. 2 Pansie
Pansie Bromfield, cynfyfyriwr o'r coleg yn Jamaica, lle bu'r bardd yn Brifathro 1965–1967.

Pansie Bromfield, a former student of the college in Jamaica, where the poet was Principal, 1965–1967.

T. 10 Ymwelwyr / Y Gwrandawr
Visitors / The Listener
Yn ystod tymor yr Hydref 1960, cipiwyd y bardd i hen Ysbyty Môn ac Arfon lle bu'n simsanu rhwng byw a marw am beth amser. Daw'r cerddi allan o'r profiad hwn.

During the Autumn term of 1960, the poet was rushed to hospital. He was seriously ill for some time. This group of poems refer to this experience.

T. 24 Offeiriad Gwlad / Country Parson
Tad y bardd yw gwrthrych y gerdd: bu yn offeiriad gwlad ym Mhenllŷn ac ym Môn am ddeugain mlynedd.

The poet's father was a Country Parson for forty years in Llŷn and Ynys Môn.

T. 26 Llwybr yr Afon / The Riverside Path
Llwybr ger afon Leri yn Nôl-y-bont. Mae'r llwybr wedi'i gau erbyn hyn, yn anffodus.

The path by the river Leri in Dôl-y-bont, the village where the poet lived. Unfortunately the path has now been closed.

T. 50 Menez Hom
Enw bryn yn Llydaw, lle bu milwyr o'r Almaen yn ymladd yn ystod yr Ail Ryfel Byd.

A hill in Brittany where a battle was fought in September 1944, the scars of which are still evident.

T. 58 Yr Ebol Prês / The Gift
Mae'r gerdd yn adrodd stori ryfeddol a ddigwyddodd i'r bardd a'i wraig ar eu mis mêl yn Norwy. Mae'r rhodd acw o hyd.

The poem describes an incident that happened to the poet and his wife on their honeymoon in Norway. The gift still sits on the mantlepiece.

T. 74 Pistyll / Waterfall
Ar gais cerflunydd o'r enw Jane Muir y cyfansoddwyd y gerdd hon, i sefyll yn gyfochrog â cherflun o raeadr hen bistyll.

This poem was requested by the sculptor Jane Muir, who wished the poem to accompany the sculpted waterfall.

T. 82 Requiescat
Cyfres o sonedau er cof am fam yr awdur.

A series of sonnets written in memory of the poet's mother. A translation of the first sonnet in Welsh is absent, and here it has been translated by the Editor.

T. 96 Darlun o'r Cyfnos / Selection from 'Evening, a Portrait'
Cerdd radio yw hon yn adlewyrchu profiad y bardd yn Jamaica.

An ode for radio, reflecting on the sounds and influences of the common society in the mid-sixties in Jamaica.